# TURN NEITHER RIGHT NOR LEFT

# TURN NEITHER RIGHT NOR LEFT

*Re-centering Evangelicalism*

Jordan Pickering

WIPF & STOCK · Eugene, Oregon

TURN NEITHER RIGHT NOR LEFT
Re-centering Evangelicalism

Copyright © 2019 Jordan Pickering. All rights reserved. Except for brief quotations in critical publications or reviews, no part of this book may be reproduced in any manner without prior written permission from the publisher. Write: Permissions, Wipf and Stock Publishers, 199 W. 8th Ave., Suite 3, Eugene, OR 97401.

Wipf & Stock
An Imprint of Wipf and Stock Publishers
199 W. 8th Ave., Suite 3
Eugene, OR 97401

www.wipfandstock.com

PAPERBACK ISBN: 978-1-5326-8022-9
HARDCOVER ISBN: 978-1-5326-8025-0
EBOOK ISBN: 978-1-5326-8028-1

Manufactured in the U.S.A.                                    APRIL 22, 2019

Scripture quotations are from the ESV® Bible (The Holy Bible, English Standard Version®), copyright © 2001 by Crossway, a publishing ministry of Good News Publishers. Used by permission. All rights reserved.

# Contents

| | | |
|---|---|---|
| Chapter 1 | Off Center • 1 | |
| Chapter 2 | Know Right from Left • 11 | |
| Chapter 3 | What the Bible Isn't • 26 | |
| Chapter 4 | What the Bible Seems To Be • 69 | |
| Chapter 5 | The Gospel Center • 108 | |
| Chapter 6 | Reading Christ • 116 | |
| Chapter 7 | Faith, Hope, and Love • 128 | |
| Chapter 8 | Faith • 131 | |
| Chapter 9 | Hope • 143 | |
| Chapter 10 | Love • 163 | |
| Chapter 11 | Centered Evangelicalism • 175 | |

*Bibliography* • 181

CHAPTER 1

# Off Center

*You shall be careful therefore to do as the LORD your God has commanded you. You shall not turn aside to the right hand or to the left. (Deut 5:32)*

POLITICS HAS ALWAYS BEEN a dirty business, and it is the greatest example of the observation made by the Preacher in Ecclesiastes:

> "Again I saw that under the sun the race is not to the swift, nor the battle to the strong, nor bread to the wise, nor riches to the intelligent, nor favor to those with knowledge, but time and chance happen to them all." (9:11)

At the moment, politicians are showing an inventiveness and vision for dirty dealing that is elevating it to a kind of artistry. With so much apparently at stake in political races, winning is imperative and the ends most surely justify the means. Giving ground to the Other Side puts us at risk. Letting them get away with an accusation here or a misdemeanor there threatens our very survival.

Take, for example, the matter of hypocrisy. Hypocrisy is always something that the Other Side does. *The Weekly Standard*[1] published an article outlining the hypocrisy of Democrats who railed against the Republican senate's plan to block President Obama's nomination of a supreme-court justice in the last year of his presidency. The author points out how many

---

1. Weekly Standard, *Great Moments*.

times Democrat-run instruments of state prevented *Republicans* from installing their preferred judges in similar circumstances.

On the other hand, *The Washington Post*[2] published an opinion piece concerning the "staggering new heights of hypocrisy" that the right has achieved in their support of Republican measures (such as wars or tax cuts or the repealing of the Affordable Care Act) that have caused the deficit to balloon—all while vilifying Democrats for any measure that would seem to increase government spending.

One would expect that having one's own hypocrisy exposed would inspire searching of heart. Surely if both sides are guilty of only caring about wrongdoing when the Other Side does it, everyone ought to realize that we have taken a wrong turn, and come back to the over-arching ideals of truth and virtue and good governance?

Obviously not. Olga Khazan[3] cites a Yale University study that points out that people so despise hypocrisy not because of the inconsistency of the hypocrite's behavior but because it reveals that their opponent isn't as virtuous as they say they are. And when *their* team is caught being hypocritical, they tend not to consider themselves accountable to the truth, but rather double-down in defense of their own "rightness." Jeff Stone, a psychology professor at the University of Arizona, observes: "They have to support the politician because the group is such an important reflection of who they are and what they believe."[4]

Polarization into right and left is dangerous because the further we retreat from our "opponents" and into our own camps, and the more these camps become part of our own identity, the more likely we are to treat them as enemies, and the less likely we are to be able to receive criticism where it is due. There is too much at stake and too much invested to allow the Other Side to score a point.

This is true in politics, but it is true in our expressions of faith too.

## Don't Turn to the Right Hand or to the Left

Deuteronomy has little to do with American politics or our tendency to polarize into warring camps. However, the call not to turn to the right hand or the left does remind us of the potential to overbalance one way or the other,

2. Waldman, *Republicans*.
3. Khazan, *Inside the Mind of a Hypocrite*.
4. Khazan, *Inside the Mind of a Hypocrite*.

rather than steadily pushing forward in a better direction, and it reminds us of the need to consider our beliefs and practices and to measure ourselves against the straight path that God has given.

For Old Testament believers, the Torah instructed Israel how to live lives of love before God and people.

> "You shall be careful therefore to do as the LORD your God has commanded you. You shall not turn aside to the right hand or to the left. You shall walk in all the way that the LORD your God has commanded you, that you may live, and that it may go well with you, and that you may live long in the land that you shall possess." (Deut 5:32–33)

However, instead of loving God and others, Israel angered God by worshiping idols and descending into injustice and hatred of the poor. Instead of living long in the land, God expelled them from it.

Many of us shake our heads at the rebellion of Israel and thank God that through Christ we are no longer idolaters and murderers of the poor. After all, where are the baals? Where are the Asherah poles? They are lost to history—dead as the wood and stone from which they were carved. And where is injustice? Christians are at the front lines of resistance against sinful policies and we are the ones championing strong families and positive values.

The bad news is this: Israel didn't worship other gods because they hated the true God or because they were an evil people. The belief in other gods and the power of these gods over various domains were consistently ingrained in the worldview of the ancient world. It was *normal*. It was a *cultural blindspot*.[5] Moreover, in the New Testament, the warnings against idolatry don't disappear; they are merely directed against, for example, the love of money—a warning that should make most of us uncomfortable.[6] And neither can we feel secure in the good fruits of our faith—Jesus' harshest words are reserved for the most righteous, well-trained and law-abiding members of the religious elite: the scribes and Pharisees. Behind all their apparent uprightness, Jesus saw hearts that lacked mercy and justice (Matt 23:23).

In other words, we can congratulate ourselves for not doing the *same things* that Israel had done, but the New Testament may well condemn us

---

5. See, for example, Jer 44:15–18, in which the people of Jerusalem blame their exile on *Jeremiah's monotheism* and their failure to keep all of the gods happy as a result.

6. E.g. Matt 6:24

for having the *same heart*. It may condemn us for unconsciously following our culture (whether liberal or conservative expressions of it), for loving money more than we love the poor, or for putting trust in our traditions while failing to live up to the weightier matters of our faith.

Turning to the right or to the left in terms of our faith is not primarily a matter of choosing between conservative or liberal theology and politics. More than this, it is a misdirection of our priorities; it is a shift from the heart of the faith as Jesus taught it, and a drift into cultural factions that may even be a *betrayal* of the faith.

## It's Us Versus Them!

Good news doesn't sell. Like it or not, people will buy a paper or click a link that says: "We're At War!" but not one that says: "Things are Going Fine!"

Warring nations require a lot of sacrifice from their people—they ask them to give up their money, their skills, and very often the lives of their sons and daughters. Such nations require propaganda to make sure that their people believe that these sacrifices are necessary. In war-time there is an argument to be made that the posters of Rosie the Riveter or Uncle Sam serve a good purpose—in conflicts of the scale of the World Wars there was too much at stake for there to be any room for grey areas and what-ifs or seeing the Other Side's point of view. But the converse is true too—negotiating the grey areas and seeing things from different angles ought to be the business of peace-time, because these are the skills that prevent wars in the first place. Being put on red alert when there isn't a war damages our ability to exercise good judgement or to think long term.

But good news doesn't sell. Reality TV with only well-adjusted contestants is boring. Every story needs a good villain, and this is no less true of the marketplace, Capitol Hill, or even your church. Media attention tends to be dominated by the sensational rather than the sensible, because so much of life is a competition for your attention and your money. It's so much easier to get both of these things from people who believe they are at war. "Our group is under attack!" "They hate your freedom!" "If we let them win, the devil wins!" "Their leader wants to steal your children!"

Life is a whole lot simpler when it's us versus them. It's much easier to secure your commitment when there's an enemy at the gate. The unfortunate result is that political platforms or Christian ministries that are built on fear tend to be heard more readily than those that are built on service of people or the attempt to comprehend and resolve complex issues.[7]

The tendency in modern church and society to split off into right- or left-leaning factions is an expression of *polarization*. When we lose our center and polarize into factions, then our task becomes the defense of our faction against incursions from the Other Side; we undervalue truth, condemn our opponents by default and we excuse a litany of errors from our own side.

Consider the following dangers of drifting from our center:

## 1. Echo Chambers

The metaphor of an echo chamber has become prominent recently, because "echo chambers" created by social-media algorithms were blamed for promoting one-sided stories about the 2016 US election and for shielding voters from diverse opinions. These algorithms were presumably written with the intention of helping users to find online pockets of community—likeminded friends—but when social-media is also the major source of news for many people, it serves only to feed users opinions that they already agree with. During the election, these algorithms weeded out conflicting viewpoints and amplified the sense of agreement with the user's own opinions, however extreme or fallacious those opinions might have been.

In 1995, long before social media existed, R. T. France criticized evangelicalism for its tendency to create circles of agreement—whether in denominations or individual churches—and then to congratulate one another for holding to orthodox theology as defined by this circle.

> "As long as one operated within the circle of those who shared these conventions [of biblical interpretation] the task was relatively painless. Others . . . who disagreed with the conventional interpretations were easily dismissed as not serious in their claim to accept the authority of Scripture, and therefore . . . constituting the 'enemy' to be refuted and opposed."[8]

---

7. You might object that *the Bible* often uses war-time imagery for the Christian life. We will return to this point, but let's for now be reminded that the Christian life concerns eternity, and so it is even more serious than war—the metaphors are important—but the *nature* of the Christian life is not militant. The Bible gives us ministries of service, peacemaking, reconciliation, love and unity.

8. France, *Women*, 12.

Because evangelicalism is (generally speaking) opposed to the idea of a state church and allows for voluntary association, it is possible for evangelical churches to divide off into various denominations or subsets of denominations if disagreements are strong enough to make co-existence uncomfortable. This tendency in evangelicalism is so taken for granted that we don't see our divisions as something that needs solving. Rather, as France observed: "We have endowed our theological and ecclesiological divisions with [a sense] of inevitability."[9] In other words, we hold stubbornly to our own views because it seems right for us to be distinct (and so to "hold onto the truth" as our faction has defined it). These distinctives serve to give each church or denomination its identity (as Baptist, creationist etc.), and for someone to question these beliefs is viewed as an act of hostility against the church itself.

We often praise the Berean church in Acts because they returned to the Scriptures to see whether what Paul taught was true. In practice, I wonder how earnestly we follow their example.

## 2. Confirmation Bias

Even when we *do* return to the Scriptures, a second danger of polarization—confirmation bias—often takes over.

Confirmation bias is "the tendency to selectively search for or interpret information in a way that confirms one's preconceptions or hypotheses";[10] in other words, we filter information according to a belief that we *already hold*. Whenever we come across information that is relevant to a certain belief, we select out only what confirms our belief and we ignore the rest.

This is a major problem with the approach to Scripture called "prooftexting"—the attempt to demonstrate that one's belief is correct by finding a handful of verses that could be seen to support it (but without checking whether there are Scriptures that oppose it).

Confirmation bias also affects how we deal with disagreement. Because we tend to congregate in communities that largely agree with us, it is very easy to assume our own rightness, and therefore to dismiss anything that doesn't conform.

John Stott was a great British teacher and theologian, and someone who loved Jesus, had the highest view of Scripture and operated easily

---

9. France, *Women*, 15.
10. Chalmers, *Cognitive Biases*, 470.

in the deep and choppy waters of biblical scholarship or in pastoral and devotional settings. Nevertheless, he held some views that I as a student disagreed with at the time. For example, he believed that women could preach to a mixed congregation under certain circumstances, and in one article he encouraged evangelicals to listen more closely to what advocates of annihilationism were actually saying.[11] How did I cope with the problem of a scholar whom I respected but occasionally disagreed with? Confirmation bias! I merely affirmed that John Stott was a brilliant theologian when his views agreed with mine, but that some flaw prevented him from being "fully biblical" when he and I disagreed.

I realize now that, irrespective of how correct Stott may or may not have been, it is the height of arrogance to use my own beliefs as a measuring stick for the orthodoxy of everyone else and simply to *filter out* and discard views different from my own.

## 3. Hostility

Confirmation bias allows us to unsee disagreeable information, but there is a common rhetorical technique called *ad hominem* (that is, an attack *against the person*) aimed at discrediting one's opponent. An *ad hominem* is not just an insult; rather, it is to engage in a personal attack in order to convince yourself or your audience that your opponent's argument cannot be trusted.

*Ad hominems* are another feature of polarization. Once we have split into factions and rooted our identity in the theology of our chosen brand, the lazy—but shockingly common—way of dealing with opponents is merely to give them a label so that our audience will know they can safely be ignored and avoided.

For example, we call one another "liberal" or "fundamentalist" or "heretic" whenever we need to deal with an uncomfortable challenge to our favorite doctrines that an "outsider" throws down. Having such a label available is enough to dismiss their view, no matter what reasons they might offer. How do we know they are wrong? Because they're on the *Other Side*.

---

11. Annihilationism is the idea that the eternity of hell refers to the inability of anyone to outlast it; it does not refer to the endless suffering of the unsaved. The judgement that God passes down to unbelievers will rather mean their annihilation—they will cease to exist—whether immediately, or after a time of punishment in proportion to their crimes.

Proper arguments are difficult, and often the evidence doesn't produce a single, clear conclusion. It is a shame that evangelicals so often fall back on the easier solution of merely labeling and out-grouping those with whom their circle disagrees, rather than engaging in frustrating but necessary discussion and risking having to change.

## 4. Specks and Planks

A final problem with polarization is that it makes us prone to hypocrisy, and hypocrisy is a clear threat to our witness to the watching world. As soon as we separate into factions and make our membership of them part of our Christian identity, it is a huge temptation to point out the faults of other factions while also excusing the faults of ours. After all, if we're at war, then we need to strike when our enemy is weak and defend ourselves when we're under attack. Being right or wrong doesn't come into it. And so we labor to show the specks in our opponents' eyes, but we aren't able to hold up the mirror and take notice of the planks in our own.

Christian involvement in US politics presents us with some interesting examples of this phenomenon—a prominent one being the Christian consensus regarding the morality of the nation's leader. Religious Americans have long demanded a high moral standard from their leaders. However, polls conducted in 2011 and 2016 found a surprising swing in the sentiments of white evangelical voters. When asked in 2011 whether they agree that "an elected official who commits an immoral act in their personal life can still behave ethically and fulfill their duties," white evangelicals were the demographic most opposed to the idea, with only 30 percent in support. In 2016, the same group was far and away the one most in favor of the same statement.[12]

---

12. Kurtzleben, *Poll: White Evangelicals.*

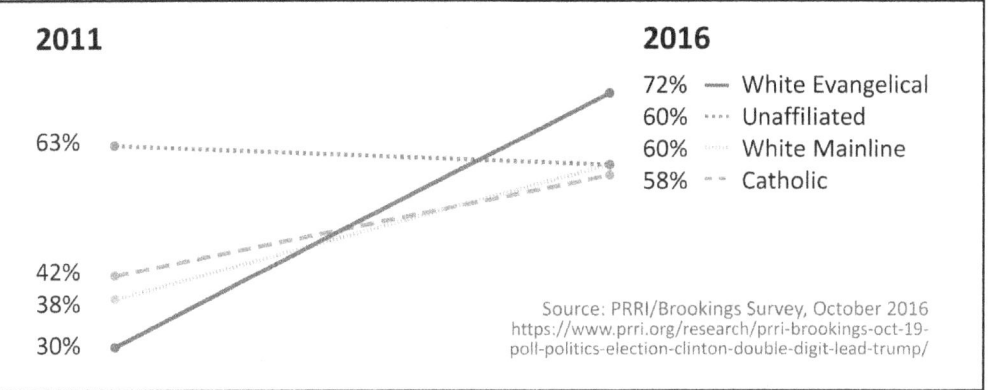

*Agreement that immorality does not disqualify a leader*[13]

This huge shift in moral outlook seems to have been motivated by the need for white evangelicals—a large percentage of whom voted for Donald Trump in 2016—to justify their support of his Republican candidacy.[14] It is notable that those who didn't have a religious iron in this particular fire (the "Unaffiliated" line) have remained at a steady 60–63 percent.

Whether the 2011 evangelicals or the 2016 evangelicals are more correct is irrelevant. The important thing is that about 40 percent of white evangelicals changed their moral stand because their political needs required them to. Public hypocrisies such as this have done serious harm to evangelical witness and eroded any moral high ground that we might seek to occupy.

Polarization leaves us comfortable in our church or denominational groups, because we have a supply of friends confirming the correctness of our own beliefs, because we can filter out evidence that "doesn't sound right," and because we can merely give pejorative labels to our opponents rather than having to deal with their arguments properly.

13. Adapted from Kurtzleben, *Poll: White Evangelicals*; original data provided by Jones and Cox, *Backing Trump*.

14. This can also be seen in the well-publicized opinion of Christian leader James Dobson who claimed that Trump made a genuine commitment to Christ (see Zylstra, *Dobson Explains*), or Wayne Grudem's (*Voting for Donald Trump*) endorsement of Trump (since retracted) not just as a necessary evil, but as a *morally good* choice.

## Turn Neither Right Nor Left

In contrast to such techniques, the Bible urges us to love our enemies and treat them as we ourselves would wish to be treated. It calls us to imitate Christ whose love for the outsider and the spiritually sick was so radical that his opponents started labelling *him*. The very least we could do to love our opponents is to properly listen to what they're saying, rather than dismissing and denigrating them.

It is true that the Bible tells us to beware of false teachers and to preserve our flock from their influence, but the same Bible also urges us to give reasons for our hope with *respect*, and it tells us to correct those who err with patience and gentleness. There is something wrong with evangelicalism that labels and outgroups and justifies its own hypocrisies while condemning the errors of others. Something needs to change.

In the next chapter, we will begin by looking at either pole of the Christian spectrum—the far right and the far left: fundamentalism and liberalism. Throwing these labels around is bad enough, but applying them inaccurately is inexcusable. Hopefully, having understood the extremes, we will be able better to see where our center ought to be.

CHAPTER 2

# Know Right from Left

*If you love those who love you, what benefit is that to you? For even sinners love those who love them. And if you do good to those who do good to you, what benefit is that to you? For even sinners do the same . . . But love your enemies, and do good, and lend, expecting nothing in return, and your reward will be great, and you will be sons of the Most High, for he is kind to the ungrateful and the evil. Be merciful, even as your Father is merciful. (Luke 6:32–36)*

EVANGELICALISM IS A BROAD movement, housing a wide spectrum of beliefs. We are united by the belief that the Bible is true and the primary authority in the Christian life, but even within such parameters there is scope for disagreement. Sadly, being gripped by the gospel has not prevented Christians from dealing very poorly with disagreement.

For example, during the Reformation—a time in which the concepts of grace and relationship with God were being renewed under the harshest persecution from the imperial church—infighting among Protestant Christians threatened their *own* survival as a church. Luther clashed with Zwingli over the matter of the Lord's Supper, and Zwingli and others clashed with the Anabaptists (re-baptizers) over the matter of baptism—to the extent that the Anabaptists were branded seditious and sentenced to death. The Zurich court decided that the best punishment for advocates of a second baptism would be to give them a *third* baptism. They were bound by hands and feet and thrown into the river to drown.[1]

We might not wish death upon those with whom we have theological disagreements, but depending on what kind of evangelical circle one is engaging with, one might be branded a "fundamentalist" if one connects the truth of the Bible too strongly with literalism, or one might be branded a "liberal" if one allows, for example, that the creation story need not be purely factual.

## Stigma Sticks!

Applying pejorative labels to one another is not just harmless banter. If we're tempted to label those with whom we disagree, we should bear in mind that it is very hard to manage what associations our hearers will have with such labels.

If you brand someone "fundamentalist," is your audience likely to understand that your target is a disciple of Jesus who is merely a little rigid in their reading of biblical genres? Or will they imagine a zealot who believes in a flat earth and is likely to gun down reproductive-health counsellors? If you brand someone "liberal," is your audience likely to understand that your target is a brother or sister who merely thinks that evolution is compatible with Genesis? Or will they imagine a resurrection denier whose plan is to brainwash their twelve-year-olds into undergoing gender-reassignment surgery?

The labels are easy to apply, but they "poison the well" against the target—in other words, the label tells your audience that whatever pours from your opponent, they had better not drink it. It gives our hearers permission to dismiss (or even vilify) someone on our say-so and without even hearing the person for themselves. This is surely the antithesis of Christian love for one's enemy.

Furthermore, as a professor of mine once said to me, "stigma sticks!" It's very hard to shake pejorative labels once they have stuck. In landmark research undertaken at Stanford in 1975, students were asked to participate in a study purported to be about suicide. Each participant was given twenty-five pairs of suicide notes, one fake and one real, and they were asked to identify which of each pair they thought was genuine. When results were

---

1. Butler, *History of Christianity*, 9.

returned, one group of students was told that they had scored extremely well and another group was told that they had done poorly.

Next, it was revealed that though the pairs of notes did indeed include one real and one fake, the students' scores were *made up*—their success or otherwise was not actually any indication of how well they had done. Now the students were asked to guess how well they had *actually* done. Though none of the students had any reason to think they had done well or badly, those who were *told* they had done well now believed that they had in fact done well, and those who were told they had failed still believed that their real score would be low. Even after students had been told unequivocally that they had been lied to, they continued to believe the lie anyway.

> "'Once formed,' the researchers observed dryly, 'impressions are remarkably perseverant.'"[2]

What this means for our categorizations of one another is this: the labels that we apply to others, once accepted by our hearers, are likely to remain in place, no matter if the facts refute us or if we ourselves retract hastily spoken words. Stigma sticks.

In offering the following descriptions of fundamentalists and liberals, I cannot hope to do as comprehensive or detailed a job as the many books already available on the subject. Nevertheless, I hope these descriptions serve adequately to outline what is at the heart of each stance, so that, if we must label our opponent, at least we can do so with accuracy.

## What is Fundamentalism?

These days, fundamentalism is associated with any form of religious extremism, unquestioning devotion to religion and holy books, and militant resistance to modernization. However, this is not what the term was originally associated with.

According to the *Evangelical Dictionary of Theology*, fundamentalism *as a movement* "arose in the United States during and immediately after the First World War in order to reaffirm orthodox Protestant Christianity and to defend it militantly against the challenges of liberal theology, German higher criticism, Darwinism and other isms regarded as harmful to American Christianity."[3] Fundamentalism as a movement was influenced

---
2. Kolbert, *Facts*.
3. McIntire, "Fundamentalism," 472.

by Princeton theologians such as B. B. Warfield, and it aimed to recover and preserve the core of the faith passed down from the Reformation. However, this is to be differentiated from fundamentalism as a *mindset*.

William Egginton[4] makes the point that "*what* one believes, while obviously important, is often not as influential on behavior as *how* one believes." While Christians from several traditions would agree that the text of the Bible is the source of the *content* of our faith, to be fundamentalist implies that one holds to this content with a certain *attitude*. "A fundamentalist," continues Egginton, "implicitly holds that what he believes corresponds to a single, underlying code that explains everything about the world, in its totality." The manner in which this is lived out tends to set fundamentalists at odds with society and those who disagree with their outlook.

While fundamentalism used to be one side of an internal church conflict—Reformation Christianity versus liberal theology—Christian fundamentalism in the latter part of the last century shifted its target towards *secular humanism*, and other facets of secular thought and practice. In other words, it is no longer merely an internal matter, but pits the church against religious *and* secular society, particularly on issues such as "evolutionism, political and theological liberalism, loose personal morality, sexual perversion, socialism, communism, and any lessening of the absolute, inerrant authority of the Bible."[5]

To accuse people of being fundamentalist, therefore, is not merely a statement about their belief in, for example, the inspiration of Scripture or its inerrancy. It implies that they exhibit a *mindset* towards the Bible and its application that makes them rigid and intolerant of those who differ from them. It is to accuse them of being over-confident in their own correctness, lacking in nuance, and blind to the effects of their own human weakness and corruption on their thinking.[6]

---

4. Egginton, *What is fundamentalism?*

5. McIntire, "Fundamentalism," 474.

6. Olson, *What is "Fundamentalism"?* He quotes Carnell who said: "[Fundamentalism] sees principles everywhere, and all principles come in clear tones of black and white."

## The Disappearance of Self-proclaimed Fundamentalists

A major complication in the task of differentiating fundamentalism from evangelicalism is that few Christians if any continue to identify themselves as fundamentalists. Olson supplies a reason for this:

> "Soon [after the media began using the term 'fundamentalist' for Iranian extremists in the late 70s], journalists and sociologists of religion were using 'fundamentalist' as a descriptor for any form of what they perceived as religious fanaticism. About the same time Jerry Falwell, a well-known American fundamentalist leader, dropped the label 'fundamentalist' and began to call himself very publicly an 'evangelical.'"[7]

This means that moderate evangelical churches ceased to be theologically distinct from those that previously identified as fundamentalist, and each movement has subsequently absorbed influences and terminology from the other. We are all united in believing in the authority and inspiration of Scripture, but it is not at all clear that we are united in how we understand these concepts. Moreover, some of the more militant and intolerant attitudes towards diversity and disagreement that usually have been associated with fundamentalism are becoming common in evangelicalism more generally—especially as the perceived threat of secular liberalizing on matters of gender and sexuality in the last decade has grown.

Olson[8] describes some of the problematic features of fundamentalism as including the tendency to:

- Confuse secondary issues with gospel issues.
- Break fellowship with fellow Christians who hold doctrines that they consider impure.
- Hunt for and expose the "heretical" beliefs of others.
- Put doctrine above ethics, so that even questionable means of defeating opponents are considered justified.
- Identify "liberal theological thinking" where it does not exist.
- Deny uncertainty in theology or interpretation.

---

7. Olson, *What is "Fundamentalism"?*
8. Olson, *What is "Fundamentalism"?*

As an example of the tendency to confuse secondary issues for gospel issues, consider the following quotes from the director of Creation Ministries International in the UK and Europe, Philip Bell:

> "The crying need for the faithful proclamation of biblical creation should hardly need highlighting. Is the Church as a whole awake on this issue? The answer is a clear and categorical no! On the contrary, there is a widespread refusal, even on the part of many professed evangelical Christians, to emphasise (or even to acknowledge) Paul's teaching. The Bible makes clear that Creation-denial ("the things that have been made," Rom 1:20) is tantamount to Creator-denial ("For although they knew God, they did not honour him as God," 1:21), and that idolatry directly follows ("because they exchanged the truth about God for a lie and worshiped and served the creature rather than the Creator," 1:25) . . . Without an understanding of the reliability and relevance of biblical creation, people will continue to languish in their ignorance, deceived and deceiving each other (2 Tim 3:13)."[9]

> "We *proclaim* Creation, not only because it is true, but because effective evangelism requires it. The Gospel of Jesus Christ is founded on an historical Adam and Eve, the serpent tempter, the taking of the forbidden fruit, and the promise of the Victor over Satan (Genesis 3:15). History's simple message—all are sinners; sin's penalty is death, spiritual and physical; Christ came to deliver us from sin's penalty and power, and from the sting and dominion of death—is *founded* on historical events recorded in Genesis."[10]

The article in the newsletter from which these quotes are taken is sent to partners of CMI—i.e., those who are already on board with creationist interpretation. The whole article is aimed at underlining for their sponsors that creationism is an essential gospel foundation, without which others are "languishing in their ignorance, deceived and deceiving each other." Bell's point is that the gospel depends on Adam and Eve's creation and fall into sin, and therefore, without creationist teaching, there is no gospel. He twice refers to *Christian* opponents as if non-creationists aren't real evangelicals—once as "*professed* evangelical Christians" and elsewhere as "*well-meaning* Christians"[11] who allegedly dishonor God by undermining creationist interpretation of the Bible's teaching on creation.

---

9. Bell, "Proclaiming Creation," 1.
10. Bell, "Proclaiming Creation," 3.
11. Bell, "Proclaiming Creation," 3.

Although CMI has been active in appealing to fellow Christians around the world for about forty years, this argument is presented as if they have never heard evangelical Christian arguments against creationist hermeneutics or cogent non-creationist explanations of Genesis and Romans, of which there are many. The argument in rebuttal of "professed evangelical Christians" is merely to read off verses from Rom 1 or Rom 5 as if their opponents must surely have never read Romans. CMI's attitude towards non-creationist Christians is one of distrust—on the border of accusing them of unfaithfulness to the gospel—and their approach to Scripture betrays the belief that their interpretation is so clear as to rule out all other interpretations.

Of course the gospel does depend on the idea that humanity is lost in sin and rebellion, and that Christ's death sets humanity on a new path—all evangelical interpretation acknowledges as much. However, whether Gen 1-3 should be read literalistically or as a more figurative genre is clearly an issue of (distant) secondary status about which evangelicals are free to disagree.

A second issue in which the influence of fundamentalism can be seen on wider evangelical theology is to do with the matter of women in ministry. Most evangelicals identify with one of two major interpretive schools. Complementarians maintain that men and women are created equal but with differences, and that these differences mean that it is God's will for men to take church leadership roles, and for women to take (equally important) support roles. Evangelical egalitarians maintain that men and women are created equal but with differences, and that these differences mean nothing in particular for the roles that men and women may occupy in the church; these should be determined according to gifts that God has allocated according to his will.

The influence of fundamentalism is not felt in the area of exegesis—each position has a credible exegetical foundation, with first-class evangelical interpreters in each camp. The influence of fundamentalism is felt in the *manner of engagement* with the position that seems more liberal (the egalitarian view).

In spite of the fact that evangelical egalitarianism has several deeply respected evangelical biblical scholars who subscribe to it, and in spite of claims that its adherents generally have been persuaded by *exegetical* evidence, many of its critics continue to insist that it is merely a Christian veneer painted on liberal feminism or secular egalitarianism.

For example, a post from John MacArthur's *Grace to You* website explicitly calls non-complementarians *syncretists* who have merely bowed the knee to feminism:

> "The legion of female pastors filling pulpits today is the legacy of the evangelical syncretists who were willing to marry feminist ideology to Scripture. That capitulation stands in opposition to the clear teaching of Scripture . . . [The passages concerning female submission and male-only leadership], read in their context, have clear universal application. In reality, no honest exegete of Scripture can come to any other conclusion."[12]

Roger Olson's complaints against fundamentalism (that it makes secondary issues into gospel issues, breaks fellowship, puts doctrine above ethics, etc.) seem harsh. Nevertheless on this issue, where fear about liberal incursions into the church on the matter of gender and sexuality runs high, each of the issues that he highlights is apparent. In the quote from *Grace to You* above, there is an accusation of heresy and a withdrawal of fellowship implicit in the term "syncretists," the basis of his opponents' theology is assumed to be liberalism, there is only a facile attempt to present his opponent's arguments in their own terms,[13] and he flat-out denies that there is any doubt that his own interpretation of Scripture is certain. Anyone who disagrees with him, he says, must be dishonest.

In summary, while the accusation that someone is fundamentalist should be avoided—especially if it is just an easy put-down that one can apply to anyone more conservative than oneself—it is important to realize that the influence of the negative qualities of fundamentalism that Olson has identified is now visible within the evangelical mainstream too.

## How Does Evangelicalism Differ From Fundamentalism?

The *Evangelical Dictionary of Theology* offers the following description of evangelicalism:

> "[Evangelicalism is] the movement in modern Christianity, transcending denominational and confessional boundaries, that

---

12. Buettel, *Evangelical Syncretism*.

13. He does directly quote both Keener and Fee, but on the basis of a short paragraph from each—without its context or the arguments that lie behind it—he dismisses their arguments as inventions or disregard for clear statements of Scripture, so that they can "kowtow to the pressures of society" and mix "God's Word with ungodly ideologies."

emphasizes conformity to the basic tenets of the faith and a missionary outreach of compassion and urgency . . . [An evangelical is] one who believes and proclaims the gospel of Jesus Christ . . . Evangelicalism is more than orthodox assent to dogma or a reactionary return to past ways. It is affirmation of the central beliefs of historic Christianity."[14]

A difference between this description of evangelicalism and Olson's description of fundamentalism is immediately apparent: evangelicalism transcends denominational and confessional boundaries, which—at least as I read it—implies that evangelicalism allows for theological difference. What unites evangelicals, however, is "affirmation of the *central beliefs* of historic Christianity." In other words, unlike fundamentalists, evangelicals ought to be very clear about what matters are central to the faith and what are secondary, and we should be united on the former and tolerant of the latter.

The *Evangelical Dictionary of Theology* also offers a brief summary of what the most important central beliefs are. Pierard and Elwell say that evangelicals believe that:

- humans are not innately good, but rebellious against God and in need of rescue (total depravity);
- salvation is made possible by Christ's atonement and through unmerited grace, not through our effort or penance;
- our task is to proclaim the gospel; and
- our hope is in Christ's return to judge and finally to set up the new heavens and the new earth.[15]

One may wish to add to the list, but it is right that the core of our faith should be centered on the person and work of Christ—the fullest revelation of God and the answer to the problem of sin and death—and Christian hope, our final destination.

By contrast, Pierard and Elwell repeat Ockenga's complaint against fundamentalism, namely that:

- it holds the wrong attitude (that of suspicion towards anyone who differs theologically);
- it practices a wrong strategy (that of separation from the world); and

14. Pierard and Elwell, *Evangelicalism*, 405, 407.
15. Pierard and Elwell, *Evangelicalism*, 406.

- it produces the wrong results (it has not turned back the tide of liberalism or had any moderating effect on it, and nor has it had a reformative influence on social issues of its day).[16]

During the era in which the distinction between evangelicalism and fundamentalism was still observed, J. I. Packer outlined the differences between these movements and liberalism in his book *"Fundamentalism" and the Word of God*. In his view, fundamentalism of the bad sort is characterized as obscurantist,[17] anti-intellectual, and anti-scholarship. It opposes new findings and treats scholarship with distrust.

Packer draws an important distinction between an evangelical reading of Scripture, which he calls "literal," and fundamentalist reading, which he calls "literalistic." He says:

> "'Literalism' is founded on respect for the biblical forms of speech; it is essentially a protest against the arbitrary imposition of inapplicable literary categories on scriptural statements. It is this 'literalism' that present-day Evangelicals profess. But to read all Scripture narratives as if they were eye-witness reports in a modern newspaper, and to ignore the poetic and imaginative form in which they are sometimes couched, would be no less a violation of the canons of evangelical 'literalism' than the allegorizing of the Scholastics was; and this sort of 'literalism' Evangelicals repudiate. It would be better to call such exegesis 'literalistic' rather than 'literal', so as to avoid confusing two very different things."[18]

He denies that the doctrine of inerrancy commits us to a literalistic reading of Scripture, claiming rather that the Bible uses various types of literature that may even present history in symbolic forms.[19] He is happy even to include the fall in Genesis as an example of history presented in a figura-

---

16. Pierard and Elwell, "Evangelicalism," 408.

17. Obscurantism is resistance to new facts or ideas, and the impulse to prevent them from becoming known. Packer (*"Fundamentalism,"* 36) warns that even evangelicals in his day sometimes fell prey to this impulse. "British evangelicals also have been heard sneering at 'the critics', making a virtue of theological ignorance, belittling scholarship and opposing 'reason' to 'simple faith' in such a way as to suggest that the purest version of Christianity is that which takes the least thought to grasp. Here, also, fear has on occasion masqueraded as faith. The one reason why Evangelicals are regarded as obscurantist is that, in fact, they sometimes are. The fault is real; we shall do well to humble ourselves because of it."

18. Packer, *"Fundamentalism,"* 104.

19. Packer, *"Fundamentalism,"* 99.

tive way—and to claim this as typical for the way that evangelicals read Scripture.[20]

In summary, the key differences between fundamentalism and evangelicalism (at least as it used to be defined) is that evangelicalism does not presume a complete theological system to which it holds with complete certainty; rather it holds to the core gospel message with certainty and shows tolerance for theological diversity on other issues.

Secondly, evangelicalism does not distrust scholarship or progress in human knowledge and biblical interpretation, and it does not insist on literalistic reading of Scripture; rather, it allows that biblical writers may have used non-literal genres in their communication of Israel's history and theology, even if this dilutes our certainty about, for example, the details and mode of creation, or what exactly happened in Israel's past.

## What is Liberalism?

The accusation that a Christian is liberal (or, from polite critics, "left-leaning") is very common, particularly as more and more younger evangelicals—who were not alive in the era dominated by battles over the "social gospel" in the church and communism in secular society—have become more interested in issues of social equality and justice. Because there is no question that the vocal concerns of the liberal political left (such as the teaching of evolution, feminism, and taxation of the rich to fund social welfare) have all been influential in prompting Christians to re-evaluate their views on creation, women, and social justice, critics feel justified in labeling such Christians liberal too.

Of course, theological liberalism is not likely to disappear any time soon, and its influence is to be guarded against. Nevertheless, there is a significant difference between *politically* liberal views and *theologically* liberal ones, and to apply such labels incorrectly can be very damaging.

Packer, writing in IVP's *New Dictionary of Theology*, describes theological liberalism as displaying the following features:

1. Liberalism is open to updating or discarding elements of faith and doctrine in favor of "advances" in science and anthropology.

2. Liberalism is skeptical of supernatural explanations for phenomena, including biblical miracles, such as the bodily resurrection of Christ;

20. Packer, "Fundamentalism," 105.

it is distrustful of beliefs transmitted by tradition, preferring reason as an overriding authority.

3. The liberal view of the Bible sees it as a human book (not divine) in which people recorded their experience of God and the world, but which is fallible and not historically reliable. As a result, churches ought not to be judgmental of the experiences of God and theologies of its members.

4. Liberalism views God as working to transform and mature human culture rather than to redeem it, and views Jesus as a model of the ideal godly person, rather than as a divine savior.

5. Liberalism is optimistic that people are naturally able to know God, and believes that all religions have true but partial perception of God. It opposes exclusive religious claims.

6. Liberalism denies the fall that brought corruption on the human race; it denies that Christ was punished in our place to atone for us, or that Christ's righteousness is imputed to us; and it denies Christ's return as the Christian hope, preferring the view that moral progress will bring about God's kingdom on earth.[21]

These sorts of attitudes can be seen in the work of liberal authors such as E. P. Sanders and Marcus Borg. Sanders describes himself as:

> "a liberal, modern, secularized Protestant, brought up in a church dominated by low christology and the social gospel. I am proud of the things that that religious tradition stands for. I am not bold enough, however, to suppose that Jesus came to establish it, or that he died for the sake of its principles."[22]

Concerning Scripture, Borg says:

> "The foundation of this way of seeing the Bible begins with the conviction that it is not the inerrant and infallible revelation of God, but the product of our religious ancestors in two ancient communities . . . the Bible is a human product: it tells us how our religious ancestors saw things, not how God sees things."[23]

---

21. Packer, "Liberalism and Conservativism," 385.
22. Sanders, *Jesus and Judaism*, 334.
23. Borg, *Convictions*, 94.

In summary, it is important to recognize that theological liberalism is naturalistic in its view of the world—it tends to deny supernaturalism, the incarnation, the atonement, and the resurrection. It does not view Christ as divine, but views him as a good moral example, and it does not view Scripture as authoritative, but only representative of the human search for meaning. For these sorts of reasons, the Princeton theologian Gresham Machen famously declared liberalism not to be a branch of Christianity, but a different religion altogether.

How Does Evangelicalism Differ From Liberalism?

From this description, it is clear that evangelicalism differs from liberalism at every turn. Why then do evangelicals continually brandish this label against their opponents?

I suspect that the main reason is *fear*—fear that the damage that liberalism has done to historical Christianity should not be repeated. The label, then, is a knee-jerk reaction to anything that would seem to cast doubt on evangelical certainties (whether they're justifiable or not), or that bears any similarity to liberal thought.

For example, the present move among some evangelicals to campaign for social justice or environmental concern is not motivated by doubts in the doctrine of God or the person and work of Christ. It is not motivated by the belief that God's kingdom must be brought about on earth. It is not accompanied by any loosening of confidence in the truth and authority of Scripture. On the contrary, it is *because of Scripture* that Christians want to see greater care for people and creation. However, because the concern for equality and social justice overlaps with the "social gospel" of theological liberalism, and because environmental concern is often linked with animism or new age, it *sounds like* old threats rearing their heads again.

## Threats to Evangelicalism

Evangelicals are rightly concerned with the preservation of the gospel and warding off errors that threaten it. Liberalism undoubtedly is opposed to the historical gospel and shifts attention—as good as it might be in the short term—to building God's kingdom on earth. Liberalism emphasizes political and social liberation above restoration of relationship with God and humanity, and above liberation from sin and death, and there is growing pressure on the church to compromise its message about sin to accommodate everyone's lifestyle choices without condemnation. It is right that the church is prepared to suffer for the truth of the gospel rather than to give up the heart of what makes us Christian.

However, with all the evangelical attention upon those leaning to the left, we must not forget that fundamentalism poses a threat too. In the political landscape, the response to the political left has been a hard swing to the right—one that has garnered much church support. The equivalent move within Christianity has been a hardening of theological positions, an elevation of disputable matters to the level of gospel truth, and a rise in hostility towards those who now appear to be siding with "the enemy."

For a religion that claims to be characterized by unity, love for enemies, and counter-cultural concern for the outsider, the swing right in the church is not a minor issue. Divisiveness, hatred, and hypocrisy are a major threat to the entire ethos of our faith and our witness to the watching world. More than this, when fundamentalist attitudes creep into historical Christianity, preaching opinion as divine truth and acting in hostility to outsiders, those in the center are left with an ever-shrinking place in the Christian world. If one is offered the false dilemma of having either to accept fringe issues as if they are the gospel or else reject the whole thing as false, what does one do? Fundamentalism risks damaging evangelism and threatening the perseverance of many of our members.

Christians are tasked with pursuing truth not presumption, being exemplars of the grace and love of Christ, showing humility, treating others better than themselves, loving enemies, aiming at gentle, restorative instruction, and being agents of reconciliation. These qualities are intended to produce recognition of our own limitations, the need to be teachable and to grow, and the need to submit to truth from wherever God chooses to reveal it—even secular sources.

Evangelicals need to withstand the threat from *both* sides. In liberalism we lose our gospel. In fundamentalism we lose our humanity. Evangelicals need to avoid *being* liberal or fundamentalist, but we also need to be cautious when applying those labels to those with whom we don't see eye to eye. Labels are often the antithesis of the Christian ethic: they are calculated to dismiss opponents without truly listening, they render us unteachable except from sources that already agree with us, and they malign our opponents in the eyes of our audience.

Evangelicalism urgently needs to recover a view of God's word and his world that gives us the ability to handle doubt and disagreement in a way that aligns with what his word teaches.

## Chapter 3

# What the Bible Isn't

*For now we see in a mirror dimly, but then face to face. Now I know in part; then I shall know fully, even as I have been fully known. (1 Cor 13:12)*

MATTHEW AND LUKE INCLUDE accounts of the devil's temptation of Jesus in the wilderness. Each records a temptation in which God's word appears on the devil's lips:

> "[The devil] said to him, 'If you are the Son of God, throw yourself down, for it is written, "He will command his angels concerning you," and "On their hands they will bear you up, lest you strike your foot against a stone."'" (Matt 4:6)

The devil quotes Scripture to Jesus in order to persuade him that the suggestion in question (to publicly and supernaturally demonstrate his messiahship at the temple) is something approved of God. Jesus, however, answers this temptation with *more Scripture*.

This seems to me to be a clash of interpretations. Both parties are using Scripture, but only one can claim to be doing so responsibly. This should stand as a serious caution for all of us, because on the back of his SUV or his Harley Davidson (or whatever his ride of choice may be) the devil could quite easily slap on a "The Bible says it, I believe it, that settles it!" bumper sticker. His deceitful appeal is proof-texted with verses of choice. It's not sufficient for a position to be "biblical"; faithful interpretation involves more than being able to marshal supporting texts.

Jesus' response to the problem is to quote a passage that stands in conflict with the interpretation that the devil gave. This, I think, is modeling an important principle in interpretation: we must not privilege too narrow a selection of biblical evidence. Jesus' answer is effectively a rebuke of interpretation that picks-and-chooses convenient evidence. Biblical arguments must appeal to a total apprehension of God's revealed plan and word.

As evangelicals, we pride ourselves in a high view of Scripture and faithful interpretation. We combine responsible scholarship with devotional submission to the claims that the word of God makes upon us. While this is our *aim*, there is a danger that we too quickly presume to have *achieved* this aim. We *know without looking* that our doctrines are secure and correct. But having texts—even lots of them—in support of our position isn't a guarantee that we've done much better than the devil did. As in Matt 4, the devil is sometimes in what has been *left out* of our doctrinal positions.

Evangelicals broadly agree that the Bible is inspired by God, perspicuous (i.e., its message is clear enough to be understood), and inerrant. However, within evangelicalism, there are a range of views of what Scripture is, how it came to be, and how it functions as God's word to us. Some evangelical views of Scripture, however, struggle to match up to the evidence with which the Bible presents us.

## Inspiration Isn't Omniscience

"If the King's English was good enough for Jesus Christ, it's good enough for the children of Texas!"

This quote is attributed to many politicians, though most often to Miriam "Ma" Ferguson who was governor of Texas in the 1920s; she allegedly said this in opposition to the idea of teaching Spanish in schools. It is, sadly, not likely that anyone said this in seriousness. It is an example of an extreme anachronism—something that is so far out of its correct time period that it becomes impossible. There was no English for Jesus to speak in the first century.

While Ferguson's "quote" might be a fake, there are persistent, thoughtless errors that are very real and not much better than this quote. I appreciate, for example, painted portraits of Jesus as a black man, not because they are an accurate representation, but because they provoke many of us to become defensive. *That's not how Jesus looked!* This is useful because it exposes our lazy assumption that Jesus looked like he looks in old European paintings—white, often blonde, often blue-eyed. While none of us knows what Jesus actually looked like, there is probably as much chance that he looked African as that he looked like a Western European. Yet this very unlikely portrait of Jesus, imposed from Renaissance Europe back onto first-century Israel, has become part of the image of Jesus that many of us hold to be right. *Jesus was like me.*

In a similar vein, our view of the inspiration of Scripture is sometimes colored by lazy assumptions that we do not interrogate. Ben Witherington tells the story of having hitched a ride with a man shortly after Neil Armstrong landed on the moon. When conversation turned to the landing and pictures of the earth as seen from the moon, the man confidently declared that it was all fake, because Revelation speaks of the angels standing on the "four corners of the earth." The earth can't be round if it has corners, and since the Bible is inspired by God, it overrules NASA's photos.[1]

The inspiration of Scripture does not mean that God spoke and people merely wrote down what he said. It *could* imply that God dictated his Bible, but it need not. It refers to the belief that God worked through the various authors and editors of the Bible so that they wrote words that God endorses as truly reflecting what he wanted to communicate. The Bible might be God's word in the sense that it is God's *direct speech*, but it might equally mean no more than that the Bible that we have is the Bible that he wanted his people to have.

When we look at what the Bible contains and what it says about itself, it is clear that the truth is somewhere between the two. The Bible is *true*, but it is also composed (for the most part) in the ordinary human way: someone was compelled to write a message to his or her readers through the genres of writing familiar to that age, and they made use of existing books, other research, and (in some cases) stages of compilation and editing. So Scripture is at the same time human and divine.

As with the divine-human nature of Christ himself, this is where the troubles begin. What does God's behind-the-scenes authorship of Scripture mean for its accuracy or the types of writing that God might use to express himself? In what way is it human?

Evangelicals tend to err on the side of affirming the *divinity* of Scripture. If the Bible is God's word, and if God is *omniscient*, it is hard to escape the conclusion that the writings of Scripture must also display God's perfect

---

1. Witherington, *Martin vs. Barton*.

knowledge. This is, however, a mistake, as the *Chicago Statement on Biblical Inerrancy* acknowledges:

> "Article IX. WE AFFIRM that inspiration, though *not conferring omniscience*, guaranteed true and trustworthy utterance on all matters of which the Biblical authors were moved to speak and write. WE DENY that the finitude or fallenness of these writers, by necessity or otherwise, introduced distortion or falsehood into God's Word."

Article VII also affirms that "the mode of divine inspiration remains largely a mystery to us."

Despite these affirmations, it is difficult to avoid picturing the Bible (as the word of God) in any other way than as if God himself were talking. But where does this leave the *humanity* of Scripture? Historically, evangelicals have denied that the dictation model of inspiration is correct. Packer says that neither evangelicals nor the early fundamentalists would have spoken about inspiration in this way.

> "The fact is that the Protestant defenders of the divine origin of the Bible during the past century have uniformly been at pains to disclaim any mechanical doctrine of the mode of inspiration, to stress that biblical authors wrote spontaneously and freely, and to insist that the product of their writing is as truly and fully human as it is divine."[2]

He adds that several of the scholars influential on the original fundamentalist movement, such as Warfield, Orr, and Hodge, even avoided the use of the term "verbal inspiration" because for God to have given the authors precise wording was too closely linked with mechanical, dictation-like ideas.[3]

Although dictation is not meant to be an evangelical model of inspiration (except in those instances where it claims to be a record of God's direct speech, for example, to Moses on Sinai), we nevertheless make arguments that are virtually synonymous with it. For example, consider the following passage from the *Evangelical Dictionary of Theology*:

> "Inspiration is not mechanical dictation; rather, the Holy Spirit guided the various biblical authors in their *selection of words and meanings* . . . Thus the words and imagery are culturally

---

2. Packer, *"Fundamentalism,"* 178.
3. Packer, *"Fundamentalism,"* 179.

conditioned, but God has nonetheless conveyed his eternal, unconditional Word through them."[4]

The authors make an effort to set "culturally conditioned" alongside his "eternal, unconditional Word," and perhaps this is sufficient to capture the mystery of divine-human Scriptures. Nevertheless, it is not obvious how "mechanical dictation" differs from "[guiding] their selection of words and meanings." How is *guiding* their words different from *giving* them their words? "Guidance" may well be suitable terminology, depending on how one intends it, but the difficulty of describing the meeting of divine and human minds in Scripture regularly leaves evangelicals with a dictation model of inspiration in practice, even if they disavow it in theory. It is very unclear how the guidance that produces God's "eternal, unconditional Word" in book form is also subject to human limitations.

In my discussions with fellow evangelicals over whether or not biblical authors exercised creative license in their storytelling, I have asked how it is that authors—often writing decades or centuries after the fact—could have come across the word-for-word dialogues spoken by their characters. Even today we don't record dialogue; our attempts at writing objective histories are limited to observable events. Historians avoid inferring things that were said behind closed doors. The answers that I have received include that "it is enough to know that it is inspired," or "God could have seen to it that that dialogues that the authors wrote lined up perfectly with what was actually said." Both of these responses seem to me to imply that the dialogues are historically accurate because God *gave the authors the words*—i.e., they were received by dictation.

Of course God was *capable* of over-riding the authors' humanity to make them mere vessels of his own words, but that is not how the Bible describes much of its own composition.[5] For example, Luke 1:1–4 claims that others "compiled a narrative of the things that have been accomplished among us," and that "it seemed good to me also . . . to write an orderly account for you." He clearly depends on Mark's Gospel (or a source common to both) for much of his material, and he implies that he used stories from other eyewitnesses of Jesus' life. Similarly, several Old Testament books

---

4. Pierard and Elwell, "Evangelicalism," 406.

5. It is also the case that God does the majority of his work on earth *through* human personhood, not in spite of it. The way that God provides, rebukes, encourages, etc. is primarily through his use of fallible people providing for, rebuking, encouraging, etc. one another.

refer by name to written sources on which they have relied, and Chronicles reuses entire passages of Kings word-for-word, making additions where appropriate.

While there clearly are predictive prophecies and the like in the Bible, and these presumably involved God giving the authors visionary access to knowledge that they did not naturally possess, most of Scripture does not present itself as oracle; it came about in very human ways, and reflects the authors' human faculties and knowledge. God did not make his authors omniscient; they wrote into their cultures and generally reflected the knowledge and types of writing available to them. God superintended somehow over the writing of his Scriptures so that their words are true, but their humanity remains.

So, we must come to terms with the divinity *and* humanity of Scripture. God is omniscient, but Scripture does not claim to be so. God evidently guided people to write histories and poems and letters that were subject to human limitations and yet nevertheless express views that he endorses as true and that he preserved for our instruction.

## Perspicuity Isn't Certainty

I recall many years ago reading a copy of the journal of a Christian apologist in which he was answering readers' questions. He was asked why he didn't seem to rely on the written works of others. His answer was that human writings, century after century, have erred and merely continued to pass around the same mistakes in each generation. He didn't see the wisdom in going to flawed human writings when he could go directly to the perfect word of God.

While at first glance this seems to be a pious and faithful thing to say, there are some glaring errors in the logic. He failed to explain how it is that human frailty had clouded the interpretations of every human author in history, but not him. If he expects only to find error in human interpretations of Scripture, why does he expect his own to be immune? Secondly, he seems not to have noticed the irony of decrying the worthlessness of human teachings *in a document intended to teach humans.*

This illustrates a common problem in Christian thinking—the idea that the Bible, as God's word, speaks directly and clearly to its reader.

Perspicuity is the name given to the idea that the Bible is sufficiently clear in its communication *of the gospel* that people are able to understand it *without the need for experts to mediate*.⁶ In other words, if a priest or a minister or a pope or a prophet were to declare some teaching to be the true gospel, "ordinary" Christians would be able to compare that teaching to the biblical gospel and be able to determine whether the expert's message is true or false. The doctrine of perspicuity does *not* intend us to imagine that the meaning of *all* of Scripture is immediately apparent to us, or that genuine understanding doesn't require hard work and responsible contextual scholarship. It merely defends against the idea that the "true meaning" of Scripture lies behind the words and is only available to an enlightened few.

Because "clarity" is often given as a synonym for perspicuity, the mistake that we make is to think that Scripture is *self-evident*—that we can merely take it on face value and its meaning and application will be obvious to us. After all, God *wants* to communicate with people, and he has given us his Holy Spirit to enable us to understand him, so why would he give us Scriptures that are *un*clear?

The attraction of this idea is not hard to see. If we are to know the truth and follow God's word to us, this is made significantly more difficult if the instructions are ambiguous or doubtful.

When I was a student, we were taught that preachers are agents of the word of God and ought to preach with confidence. There might well be more than one interpretation of a text, but we ought to establish what seems to be the best interpretation and preach it with conviction. We know that Christ is the answer, so why undermine that by seeming unsure? We mustn't show doubts and uncertainties from the pulpit.

Certainty is attractive because it is easy to confuse it for truth. Nobody is likely to believe your answers to life's questions if *you yourself* seem not to believe them. Conversely, if you speak with conviction, people are more likely to be persuaded that what you say is true. It is better, therefore, to take Scripture at face-value, because the preacher can be confident, and the hearers can be encouraged by Scriptures that speak clearly to them.

Look again at the conviction with which Buettel proclaims the theological position of his constituents:

---

6. "All things in Scripture are not alike plain in themselves, nor alike clear unto all; yet those things which are necessary to be known, believed, and observed, for salvation, are so clearly propounded and opened in some place of Scripture or other, that not only the learned, but the unlearned, in a due use of the ordinary means, may attain unto a sufficient understanding of them." (*Westminster Confession of Faith*, Chapter 1.7)

> "That capitulation stands in opposition to the clear teaching of Scripture . . . In reality, no honest exegete of Scripture can come to any other conclusion [than ours]."[7]

With such clarity and with such high stakes—syncretism no less—it is hard to imagine anyone in *Grace To You* circles daring to ask whether evangelical egalitarians don't perhaps, just maybe, have a point. To disagree with the teacher is to deny Scripture itself.

The great problem with belief in the absolute clarity of Scripture (rather than sufficient clarity limited to the gospel core) is that Christians teaching on the same issue come to a variety of conclusions, often in contradiction with one another. The Bible does not produce consistent interpretations:

> "It seems to be the case that the more you insist that you are based on the Bible, the more fissiparous [divisive] you become . . . the church splits up into more and more little groups, each thinking that they have got the biblical truth right."—N. T. Wright

> "I speak to those with a high view of Scripture: it is very distressing to contemplate how many differences there are among us as to what Scripture actually says . . . The fact remains that, among those who believe the canonical sixty-six books are nothing less than the Word of God written, there is a disturbing array of mutually incompatible theological opinions."—D. A. Carson[8]

Christian Smith[9] draws attention to the popular evangelical book format, in which theology is presented by means of a discussion of "three views on [x]," "four views on [y]," and so on. At the time of writing his book in 2011, he identified thirty-four such titles, plus a book that listed multiple views on seventeen topics. By his calculation, this produces *five million* possible variations of evangelicalism, all reading the same Bible as the word of God. It will also not do to dismiss such problems as related to "matters of dispute"—those of secondary importance to the faith. He points out that the disagreements cover such topics as inerrancy, providence, creation, predestination, the image of God, Christology, atonement, justification, sanctification, baptism, the Lord's Supper and many others. He concludes:

> "On important matters the Bible apparently is not clear, consistent, and univocal enough to enable the best-intentioned, most

---

7. Buettel, *Evangelical Syncretism*.
8. These quotes are cited in Smith, *Bible Made Impossible*, 18.
9. Smith, *Bible Made Impossible*, 22–25.

> highly skilled, believing readers to come to agreement as to what it teaches. That is an empirical, historical, undeniable, and ever-present reality."

In these various disagreements, it is obvious that not all of us can be right, and yet (at least in some evangelical circles) you wouldn't detect any hint that the leading voices are anything but certain of their own interpretations. Some of the views on a given Christian issue may—when the veil is peeled back and Christ calls an end to history—prove to have been the correct ones. Although some of these confident teachers will indeed have been teaching true ideas, to have claimed with certainty that theirs was the authoritative answer when they could not possibly have known would still represent *false teaching*. False confidence is not better for the church than legitimate uncertainty.

Those who still would rescue God's word from the claim that it is frequently unclear sometimes say, as was once said to me: "The Bible is clear; it's people who are not!" That's all very well; the effects of the fall upon our thinking clearly do impair our ability to perceive spiritual truths. But the problems with understanding Scripture are not limited to spiritual blindness or the captivity of our minds to sin. More to the point, the Bible is God's post-fall word to a lost people—it is *for* fallen people. For whom is it clear if not for us? If a number of the Bible's doctrines and details are only dimly perceptible to us, it's because God wanted it that way.

## Inerrancy Isn't Factuality

In 1983, a controversy over Robert Gundry's commentary on Matthew came to a head at a meeting of the Evangelical Theological Society (ETS). Gundry claimed that certain events and sayings of Jesus were at least partially constructed by Matthew and were not fully historical. He wrote:

> "Hence, 'Jesus said' or 'Jesus did' need not always mean that in history Jesus said or did what follows, but sometimes may mean that in the account at least partly constructed by Matthew himself Jesus said or did what follows."[10]

> "Comparison with the other gospels, especially with Mark and Luke, and examination of Matthew's style and theology show that

---

10. Gundry, *Matthew*, 630.

## What the Bible Isn't

he materially altered and embellished historical traditions and that he did so deliberately and often."[11]

Gundry's point is not that the Gospel of Matthew is *fictional*—he sees integral connection between the story and the events of history—but he is arguing that the story and history are not necessarily *identical*. Because this implies that parts of Matthew didn't really happen, opposition to Gundry in evangelical circles began to grow. He did not agree that his views implied that the Bible is untrue or that they were incompatible with the doctrine of inerrancy. He wrote:

> "I do not deny that events reported in the Bible actually happened, but only that the biblical authors meant to report events, or historical details in connection with events, at points where Geisler and others think they did so mean. I deny in some texts what would be the literal, normal meaning for a reader who assumes a modern standard of history-writing, but not what I believe to be the literal, normal meaning for the original audience, or even for a modern audience that is homiletically oriented."[12]

In other words, Gundry claimed to be arguing that Matthew's Gospel *does* record real events, but at least partially in a genre of writing that was not written or read as merely factual. He argued that the genre is *midrash*—a creative form of Jewish commentary, common to the religious thought life of that day. Midrash is an ancient method of explaining or elaborating upon biblical texts by adding imaginative story episodes to fill gaps in the text.

> "Historically, rabbis wrote midrash to explain parts of the biblical text that aren't clear. If there seemed to be a missing piece to a story, an inconsistency between two different passages, or a redundant word or verse, the rabbis would explain the problem by writing a new midrash, filling in the missing dialogue, reconciling the seeming contradiction, or showing how there is no redundancy since each word is there to teach a different lesson or practice."[13]

As an example of midrash, the *Jewish Women's Archive* offers the story of Abraham smashing the idols in his father's house. It is an event presented as if it is historical, but it would nevertheless have been understood by readers as a tale to suggest, purely by speculation, why God might have chosen

---

11. Gundry, *Matthew*, 639.
12. Quoted by Merrick and Garrett, "Introduction," 11.
13. Jewish Women's Archive, *Telling Stories*.

Abraham rather than someone else—something that the Torah doesn't explain.

Gundry pointed out that the use of midrash *would* imply falsehood if one were reading the text with the assumption that the genre is modern history, but since ancient readers were familiar with midrash but *unfamiliar* with our journalistic idea of history-writing, they would not have assumed that Matthew was only allowed to write precisely "what happened." The *normal reader* in the ancient world, in Gundry's opinion, would have understood that they were reading literature that allowed for creative input by the author.

In spite of this explanation, and seemingly without any attempt from his opponents to answer it, Gundry's comments were taken to imply that the Bible exhibits features that are not factually historical and therefore are *untrue*. Norman Geisler, who spearheaded the opposition to Gundry, insisted that it is unevangelical to hold such beliefs and that it is against the consensus about inerrancy that ETS members held. He wrote an appeal to ETS members saying:

> "ETS is not merely a theological debating society. By its very name it is the 'Evangelical Theological Society'. Besides this unspoken consensus on evangelical theology, the Constitution spells out an explicit, undebatable 'doctrinal basis' which confesses 'the Bible in its entirety is the Word of God written, and therefore inerrant in the autographs."[14]

At the ETS meeting that year, members took a vote over whether Gundry should be asked to resign from the society and the motion passed with a 74 percent majority. Gundry resigned.

## What is Inerrancy?

The fact that there is a book called *Five Views on Biblical Inerrancy* should already alert us not to assume that the contours of the doctrine are obvious. If there was a consensus concerning inerrancy when Geisler wrote to the ETS, it seems as though there isn't one now.

Article XII of the *Chicago Statement on Biblical Inerrancy* connects inerrancy to "being free from all falsehood, fraud, or deceit." As is obvious from the Geisler-Gundry controversy, while we agree that the Scriptures do

---

14. Geisler, *ETS Vote on Robert Gundry*.

not intentionally mislead or present untruths, what constitutes falsehood in literature is not always clear.

A definition from Norman Geisler's fold reads as follows:

> "Inerrancy simply means that the Bible is without error. It's a belief in the 'total truthfulness and reliability of God's words' . . . Jesus said, 'Your word is truth' (John 17:17). This inerrancy isn't just in passages that speak about salvation, but also applies to all historical and scientific statements as well. It is not only accurate in matters related to faith and practice, but it is accurate and without error regarding any statement, period (John 3:12)."[15]

Evangelicals agree, I think, that inerrancy at least means that the Bible is *true*. John 17:17 seems to secure that. However, in expanding upon what is meant by truth, they add that the Bible is "accurate and without error regarding any statement, period." This is where things become difficult.

The doctrine of inerrancy comes with a long list of exceptions that (it is claimed) do not invalidate the rule—in other words, there technically *are* errors but we still believe that the Bible is inerrant. For example, 1 Kgs 4:26 says that Solomon had forty-thousand horse-stalls, whereas Chronicles says it was four thousand. This is a clear contradiction, but such mistakes are usually explained as problems in the *copying* of texts. Inerrancy only applies to the *autographs*—the original documents that God inspired, but which are lost to us. Although we can't know for sure, we believe they did not include such mistakes.

Or consider statements such as "the sun rose"; this is factually false, because the earth spins, the sun doesn't rise. Nevertheless, this is not an *error*, because the Bible uses ordinary human language that is accommodated to our experiences. But can ordinary human language be described as *accurate* with regard to science? Accurate "regarding any statement, period"? How do we judge the truth and accuracy of *poetic* statements?

Consider Ps 104:5.[16] The psalm talks about the earth being set on foundations so that it can't be moved—an historical event (creation) that relates to matters of science (the cosmos). Is it an *accurate* statement of historical and scientific fact that the earth is fixed upon foundations? If we assume that the psalmist was speaking figuratively, rather than just describing the cosmos as he understood it, perhaps we can say that such statements don't need to be factually accurate *because this is poetry*. But this is to say that a

---

15. Defending Inerrancy, *What is Biblical Inerrancy?*
16. "He set the earth on its foundations, so that it should never be moved."

statement of historical and scientific relevance is able to be factually *inaccurate*, but—because the genre rules allow it—nevertheless true.

This introduces yet another problem: we are comfortable with the idea that poetry can take license with facts, and so we don't expect poetic truth to be literal and factual. We are *not* comfortable with "poetic license" from authors writing *narratives* about Israel's past. But these are *our* expectations of texts. How do we know that ancient readers shared our assumptions? If poets were allowed to sidestep fact in their telling of the past, on what grounds are the Bible's storytellers *not* allowed?

It seems as though inerrancy depends very heavily on how ancient genres intended to communicate truth and history—something that J. I. Packer underlined for us years ago.

*Packer on Inerrancy*

Packer was one of the lead theologians responsible for drafting the *Chicago Statement on Biblical Inerrancy* in 1978 and the *Chicago Statement on Biblical Hermeneutics* in 1982. According to Geisler,[17] Packer continues to affirm his commitment to the Chicago Statements and to his belief that Gundry-like views of Scripture are in violation of these statements.

However, his views expressed in *"Fundamentalism" and the Word of God* in the late 50s are much more open to the possibility of non-literal events in Scripture than his strong support for the comparatively rigid Chicago Statements would seem to suggest.

Firstly, the younger Packer argues that we need to judge truth in terms of what *claims* the passage is making, and that genres that rely upon non-literal modes of communication will vary in how certain we can be about what those claims are:

> "The question which the interpreter must constantly ask is: what is being *asserted* in this passage? The more poetic, imaginative and symbolic the form in which the truth is presented, and the further the truth transcends our present experience and comprehension . . . the harder it is to answer that question with exact precision . . . This is just to say that the infallibility and inerrancy of Scripture are relative to the intended scope of the Word of God."[18]

---

17. Geisler, *Packer Stands Firm*.
18. Packer, *"Fundamentalism,"* 97–98.

Secondly, he is *critical* of views of the Bible's narrative that insist it should be read as factual reports. Rather, he claims, to take the text literally is to read it *as literature*, following the rules of its genres.[19]

Finally, Packer acknowledges that biblical narratives sometimes *represent history* in symbolic forms. To liberals who accused evangelicals of failing to understand that the Bible's stories are speaking symbolically, Packer responds that evangelicals *do* recognize that historical events can be communicated in figurative language, but this does not mean it isn't nevertheless a true (though non-literal) picture of history:

> "Those who take this line upbraid Evangelicals for being insensitive to the presence of symbolism in Scripture. But this is not the issue. There is a world of difference between recognizing that a real event (the fall, say) may be symbolically portrayed, as Evangelicals do, and arguing, as these persons do, that because the fall is symbolically portrayed, it need not be regarded as a real event at all, but is merely a picture of something else. In opposing such inferences, Evangelicals are contending, not for a literalistic view, but for the very principles of biblical literalism which we have already stated—that we must respect the literary categories of Scripture, and take seriously the historical character of the Bible story... We must allow Scripture to tell us its own literary character, and be willing to receive it as what it claims to be."[20]

So, it would seem that the younger Packer was opposed to the sort of literalism that reads the Bible as if it were eye-witness journalism, and affirmative of the idea that true history can be communicated in figurative forms—it is important that we assess what truth claims are being made in terms of the genre rules of the literature in question.

He viewed inerrancy in a way that most or all of the evangelical world can agree on—it is a claim about the *truth* of what we find in Scripture, but not a claim about *what sort of information* we ought to find in Scripture. Our interpretation ought to depend on the characteristics of the literature that we find there; the genres of literature in the Bible don't depend on the kinds of texts we'd prefer to be there.

This would seem to be in contrast with the views that Geisler (and seemingly Packer too) expressed in the Gundry controversy—a view that seems to me to be a serious misstep.

---

19. Packer, *"Fundamentalism,"* 104.
20. Packer, *"Fundamentalism,"* 105.

## Geisler's Mistakes

Gundry's view on Matthew might well be incorrect, or at least under-supported by clear evidence. Perhaps his views *do* take him dangerously far from historical Christianity. Whatever Gundry's status might be, the response from Geisler and others involves serious errors of its own. Firstly, it confuses history, truth, and fact. Secondly, it appeals repeatedly to *tradition* rather than addressing the argument or consulting Scripture—an approach to conflict that falls far short of historical Christianity too.

### *History, Fact, and Truth are not Directly Related*

Q: Is metaphor true or false?

Q: Is history true or false?

These questions both appeared on a quiz that I used to give my students in a module on biblical narrative. The questions are supposed to induce puzzlement, because to apply true-false categories to genres of history or to literary devices is a poor fit.

The attempt to classify metaphor as true or false is more obviously wrong. Metaphors might be bad or good, or appropriate or inappropriate, but they are not true or false. One may use a good metaphor in service of a falsehood, or one may try to illustrate something that is true with an inappropriate metaphor.

For example, I have a friend who, in preaching class, tried to illustrate a point about the redemptive shedding of Christ's blood. He chose the metaphor of *cutting oneself shaving*. There was some forgotten point of connection that made it less ridiculous than it now sounds, but it was nevertheless a thoroughly inadequate comparison. It was a bad metaphor.

The question of whether history is true or false should equally seem to be the wrong question to ask, and yet it exposes a lazy assumption that many people hold about the nature of history. We assume that history is about facts, and if the facts are correct, then it is true.

I grew up under the latter part of the *Apartheid* regime in South Africa, and subject to all the deceitful and cruel propaganda of the nationalist government. Black people were prevented from getting a decent education or occupying high-profile jobs or government positions—and then this was used as evidence that they were too stupid to govern or to work at a high level. Except for those who worked as servants, black people were kept out of white areas and out of the public eye.

Our school history lessons focused on white settlement, the Great Trek, and the wars fought by whites, particularly those against the black nations. A favorite story was the massacre of Piet Retief and his hundred-member delegation of Afrikaner settlers, who had negotiated a land treaty with the Zulu king Dingane. The settlers were invited to a celebration of the agreement, at which Dingane ordered the delegation to be taken captive, and they were killed and their bodies left to wild animals. This atrocity was presented in such a way that portrayed black people as brutal and untrustworthy, and the Retief delegation as noble and innocent victims. In other words, many of our school history lessons amounted to white-supremacist propaganda.

The history of whites in South Africa was taught to us from the perspective of European colonization as a rightful claim on the land. Europeans—as always seems to be the case—found the land largely "empty," and they *graciously* shared their improvements and advancements with the uncivilized, unwashed tribes.[21]

While the textbooks were clearly *historical*, and while they clearly communicated several facts, *Apartheid* teaching could not be accused of being *truthful*. Its truth value was not established by either its historicity or its factuality; it needed not depart from the facts at any point (though I am sure it frequently did). The biased *selection* and *framing* and *interpretation* of fact and history were enough to render it untrue.

By contrast, Jesus' parables might easily read as the telling of historical events—the Good Samaritan, for example, could easily be an accurate retelling of a past event—and yet they need no connection to the real past at all. We assume that most of them are not factual stories, or that they are only loosely based on real events. Nevertheless, none of us accuses Jesus of lying—truth does not depend on fact or history in all circumstances. There is no necessary connection between the two.

None of us ought to be confused by these things. Presumably all of us were once guilty of telling our parents the truth, the partial truth and nothing but the convenient truth.

History is neither fact nor truth. History is the word we use for interpretation of the past.[22] These stories may lie about the evidence, or they may

---

21. This should be read with deep sarcasm, in case that isn't obvious.
22. I acknowledge that we often use "history" to mean the events of the past itself.

tell lies of omission by presenting only *some* of the facts, or they may present all the known facts but nevertheless skew the interpretation to favor a false conclusion. We have daily examples from the news of political analysis from left and right that examines the same events and comes to opposite conclusions.

History can be true or false depending on its purpose and the degree to which the required sort of evidence meets that purpose. But history itself is not true. There is no such thing as a true or a false *genre*.[23]

## Gundry, Geisler and Truth

Gundry argued that parts of Matthew's Gospel are midrash (and not necessarily historical) but nevertheless true. He insisted that this doesn't contradict inerrancy because this genre doesn't purport to be factual. Geisler, on the other hand, viewed this genre to be unbecoming of a book that is the word of God. Geisler's argument was that Gundry's *stated beliefs* might conform to the doctrine of inerrancy, but in practice his interpretation of biblical texts proved that he doesn't:

> "Gundry's is a *de facto* denial of inerrancy, for he denies that some events reported in Scripture did in fact occur. But our ETS statement insists that we believe the entire Bible is true."[24]

Twenty years later, Geisler repeated the same view:

> "While Gundry confesses to believe that the Bible is the inerrant Word of God, he denies that these events reported by Matthew are literally and historically true. But to deny that what the Bible reports in these passages actually occurred is to deny in effect that the Bible is wholly true."[25]

To accuse Gundry of treating the Bible as *untrue* betrays the confusion of history, fact and truth. Evangelicals agree that the Bible is *true*, but Geisler assumes that its truth means that it is "*literally* and *historically* true." Consider even the phrase "events reported by Matthew." This is begging the

---

This is not what is under discussion here.

23. "'Historicity' is not a genre—it expresses a belief in the reality of what has been presented. But of course, reality can take many literary forms." (Walton, "Historical Adam," 242)

24. Geisler, *ETS vote on Robert Gundry*.

25. Geisler, *Methodological Unorthodoxy*.

question—it assumes that the purpose of the text is to report facts about the past, but the purpose of the Gospels is precisely the matter that is under examination in this controversy. To say that Matthew is *reporting events* is to presumptuously assign Matthew a genre that by definition excludes Gundry's view. This is something that must be *demonstrated*, not assumed.

The purpose of literary genres determines in large degree what relationship to fact they are required to have. Modernist history-writing purported to be objectively recording what happened in the past. Such a genre requires a high degree of correspondence to fact, because the purpose is to present facts. However, it is an error to imagine that the purpose of all accounts of the past must be to tell "what happened." Over the last number of decades, it has become more and more apparent that objectivity doesn't exist—at least not in humans. All history is selective and interpretive and very much bound to the limitations and prejudices of the historian. Nevertheless, the popular assumption that all history is for finding out "what happened" has been very difficult to shed. There are many genres that retell events of the past that are not intended to be factual reports. In storytelling, the purpose of recounting the past might be, for example, to entertain—and in such cases it matters that the story is entertaining, not that it perfectly corresponds what actually happened. The embellishments of the storyteller are not *false*, because the purpose is not to present the facts.

My wife enjoys telling a good story, but due to a personality flaw of mine (and especially when the story reflects on me in some way) I can't stop myself from interrupting her and relentlessly and annoyingly correcting the facts. Once she's stopped being irritated, she reminds me that she is telling our friends how the story *felt* and in full Technicolor. The facts are not the point—the gist of it will do.

Consider also your pastor. If he's like most pastors, he likes to open some of his sermons with a joke. However, although the joke was found on the internet (and was likely never a real event in time), the pastor might start telling the joke as though it were something that happened *to him*. After an eternity, the punchline eventually comes and we all realize that this was a set-up. Although he is speaking from the pulpit and telling something that happened to him that didn't *really* happen, no one is offended or accuses him of "bearing false witness." It is in the nature of the genre that the audience needs to be misled so that the punchline is unexpected and therefore (occasionally) funny.

This is precisely the sort of point that Gundry was attempting to put across to his evangelical colleagues. He argued that Geisler was demanding a (now debunked) modern standard of history-writing from ancient writers who had no reason to subscribe to such standards and who may have been writing in a genre that bears little relation to modernism's supposedly objective, journalistic type of history-writing. Geisler's response amounted to the charge that some genres are *inherently false*, and it would be inappropriate for these to be in our Bible, but this is merely to double down on his view of what history *ought to be*.

It is understandably difficult to accept that God might have allowed his inspired Scriptures to be less than fully factual,[26] because we have been so well drilled firstly to think of history as facts, and secondly to think of the biblical narratives as history. But truth, fact, and history are different and should be kept distinct.

Gundry may be wrong about the genre of Matthew, but he is right that we can't tell God what genres He is allowed to have spoken through.

*Unchristian Approach to Conflict*

Geisler's first mistake concerns inerrancy itself—he assumes that the Bible's narratives are history, and he assumes that history is true because it is factual. Neither of these assumptions is likely to be correct.

Geisler's second mistake is to do with his handling of the conflict itself. Why is someone's handling of conflict important to the doctrine of inerrancy? It is important because the way in which the doctrine is defended reveals something about its biblical basis.

Fearmongering and Failure to Listen

Geisler has regularly found reason—since 1983—to repeat his charge that Gundry and others like him are implying that the Bible is *untrue*, in spite of their claims to the contrary. It is another example of the problem with which this book began: evangelicals tend to be over-confident in the rightness of their own positions and suspicious of those who differ.[27] So instead,

---

26. Again, this is not to say that Scripture is ever *untrue* or even *unhistorical*; just that its genre of storytelling isn't necessarily *about the facts*.

27. We most likely fall prey to cognitive biases—i.e., common patterns of thinking that are biased in the favor of the thinker. Confirmation bias is one that causes us to

we shut down conflict by vilifying our opponent, excluding them by an exercise of force, and warning our own camp about what might happen to *them* if they follow our opponent's example. I struggle to see how this shows other-centered love for one's enemies.

The following quotes come from Geisler's *Defending Inerrancy* site where statements such as the following decorate most pages:

> "We're In Serious Danger! Evangelical Christians have historically believed the Bible to be the Word of God. However, we're witnessing a departure from this foundational view. We are trying to raise awareness before it's too late."
>
> "Standing up for the Bible before it's too late! This is why the *Defending Inerrancy* initiative was created. We've already lost a growing list of evangelical scholars over the issue of inerrancy. Now we are trying to reach the latest generation of Christian leaders before it is too late."[28]

Raising these sorts of alarms is good when there are genuine threats to salvation, but the appeal here is based on a faulty view of truth and history, and proclaimed as though there isn't legitimate variation within the evangelical world in terms of how inerrancy is understood. The idea that "a growing list of evangelical scholars" is being "lost" would seem to me to imply that their faith itself is in jeopardy, and that if the next generation were to begin believing that perhaps the old view of inerrancy is inadequate to explain the phenomena of the Bible, then it would somehow be "too late."

This language is merely manipulative in its attempt to persuade you—without argument—of their own viewpoint, and to compel your conformity lest you should be "lost" too.

The problem with this approach is that it does not model the evangelical approach to Scripture that it claims to be defending—instead of making a clear case from the Bible's teaching, they apply peer pressure, and instead of encouraging Christians to test their doctrines against Scripture,

---

read the Bible or the views of others with a filter that fits the evidence into beliefs that we already hold, and we tend not to notice evidence that doesn't fit, or we quickly explain it away. Another common bias is the False Consensus Effect, in which people see "their own behavioral choices and judgments as relatively common and appropriate to existing circumstances while viewing alternative responses as uncommon, deviant, or inappropriate" (Chalmers, *Cognitive Biases*, 472). This means that we are convinced that there is wide agreement with our view, whether in the evidence of Scripture or in a group such as a church or denomination, which means that views that differ from ours are fringe, deviant or even a threat to the group.

28. Defending Inerrancy, *What is Biblical Inerrancy?*

they spell doom for anyone who disagrees. The *Bible* is our authority, not our doctrines. Evangelicals repudiate systems of Christian authority that put tradition or reason or authoritative teachers above the Bible, and like it or not, doctrine grows as understanding grows. Doctrine is human reason systematizing the Bible's teaching and encoding it into tradition. It is not the Bible.

## Appeal to Tradition

What is most striking about the Gundry-Geisler controversy—and this conflict is far from unique in this regard—is that the evangelicals allegedly defending against the erosion of the Bible's authority made little or no effort to argue from the Bible. The appeals that Geisler made were consistently to *tradition*. Consider two examples from his original appeal to the ETS:

> "Besides this unspoken consensus on evangelical theology, the Constitution spells out an explicit, undebatable 'doctrinal basis' which confesses 'the Bible in its entirety is the Word of God written, and therefore inerrant in the autographs.'"[29]

Here Geisler argues that Gundry ought to be expelled because there is an evangelical *consensus* on what inerrancy means and an *undebatable* doctrinal basis that humans have written into their constitution.

> "Good hermeneutics demand that we exclude Gundry from our membership. For the issue boils down to how we are to interpret the ETS constitution and doctrinal basis. 1) Will we interpret them as the authors meant them? 2) Or, will we interpret them for what they mean to us? In short, if we approach the ETS statements the way 'evangelical' and 'conservative' scholars (which we claim to be) have historically approached the Scriptures, then we must reject Gundry's view of Scripture as unorthodox. Certainly it is not in accord with the 'evangelical' view of inerrancy (as envisioned by the ETS founding fathers) to deny the historicity of sayings or events reported in the Gospel record."[30]

It is ironic that Geisler claimed that our hermeneutics require us to interpret texts according to authorial intention, because this is precisely what *Gundry was doing* in arguing that Matthew intended his Gospel to be read

29. Geisler, *ETS vote on Robert Gundry*.
30. Geisler, *ETS vote on Robert Gundry*.

(in parts) as midrash. Geisler, on the other hand, was making a philosophical claim (truth cannot be communicated by certain genres of literature), not an exegetical one.

More to the point, notice how he supports his accusation of error in Gundry's work by appealing to the ETS constitution, how conservatives have "historically" approached the Scriptures, and the "'evangelical' view of inerrancy" envisioned by the "founding fathers." The main impetus of the Protestant Reformation was to "return to the sources," namely Scripture, and to reject the notion that church tradition is our primary authority. Up to that point, the Catholic Church had taken on the role of mediator between man and God, and the word of the Pope and decisions of their councils were given divine authority. What the church authorities taught as God's divine will was taken as such. The Reformers pointed out how often popes and councils contradicted themselves, and they declared that *Scripture* was authoritative over the human teachings of the church.

The ETS is proud of its claim to be guardian of historical Christianity, and yet, while the Reformers urged us to keep returning to Scripture and to keep reforming, it was *Gundry* arguing that we need to relook at Scripture and Geisler arguing that the traditions won't allow it.

The appeal to tradition is attractive because it provides a shortcut. Often one doesn't have to prove that one is right; one just has to *win the group* by insisting on the traditions to which it already subscribes.[31] Tradition provides a means of appearing biblical and appearing to be defending the faith-once-delivered because it appeals to the familiar. But no-one got closer to the truth by refusing ever to move.

## Is Inerrancy Biblical?

Inerrancy is a doctrine about *the nature of the Bible*, and seeing as the Bible is a collection of books written over centuries, it is not a surprise to find that there is no book or passage that sets out to explain to us what the Bible is.

---

31. Chalmers (*Cognitive Biases*, 474, 476) identifies other cognitive biases that might be at play here. In-Group Bias is "the tendency for people to give preferential treatment to others they perceive to be members of their own group," which means that we tend to trust our own kind rather than making a neutral inquiry into the truth of the matter. The second bias is called Illusory Truth Effect, which is "the tendency of people to identify a statement as true simply because they have heard it before, irrespective of its actual truthfulness." This predisposes us to favor status-quo views as more likely to be true—because we've heard them before.

So the doctrine of inerrancy is inferred from texts in Scripture concerning the nature of God and his revelation to us.

For example, we are confident that the Bible is *true* because:

- In John 17:17, Jesus says: "Sanctify them in the truth; your word is truth." It is fair to say that if the Bible is God's word, then it must be true.
- A very common synonym for the gospel message in the epistles of Paul, James, and John is "the truth." For example, Col 1:5 says: "Of this [hope] you have heard before in the word of the truth, the gospel."[32]
- Second Timothy says: "Do your best to present yourself to God as one approved, a worker who has no need to be ashamed, rightly handling the word of truth" (2:15). This again refers to the gospel message, apostolic teaching and (most likely) to the Scriptures that were recognized as God's word by that time. It is clear that Paul regarded such things as truth to be handled faithfully.

So, the *truth* of Scripture is quite securely established, and thus the more general definition of inerrancy as "wholly true" is defensible. Elaborations upon the definition, such that terms like "factual" and "accurate in matters of science and history" get added, are much less clearly supportable from Scripture.

*Defending Inerrancy* attempts to defend the idea of total accuracy in every statement in this way:

> "It is not only accurate in matters related to faith and practice, but it is accurate and without error regarding any statement, period (John 3:12)."[33]

The cited text, John 3:12, reads:

> "If I have told you earthly things and you do not believe, how can you believe if I tell you heavenly things?"

This clearly does not directly mention inerrancy, or even Scripture, but the argument seems to be that Jesus—the Word of God—spoke about both

---

32. Of course, "the gospel" is the message of salvation (Eph 1:13) and does not necessarily mean the whole of Scripture, but it is reasonable to infer that God's word is true more generally.

33. Defending Inerrancy, *What is Biblical Inerrancy?*

heavenly and earthly matters, so the Bible as the word of God is also able to be the divine word even on earthly matters.

No one is likely to question the idea that if God *dictated facts* from heaven, they would be completely without error. But this is to beg the question—the authors are requiring us to accept that the Bible's divinity means that it must be factual, yet this is exactly the issue that is being debated. The Bible is *not* God's dictation from heaven; it is divine-human literature. Many past scholars readily admitted that it is not certain how this dual nature of Scripture works in practice—they were happy to admit there is a sense of mystery about inspiration.[34] Secondly, it is a long way from certain that the Bible intends us to read it as facts. The big question in this debate is: to what degree are the genres that we have in the Bible bound to fact and history? Are Gen 1–11 or Job or Jonah *untrue* or *in error* if they turn out to be not strictly historical?

To say that God directed the biblical writers to write factually about earthly things is to assume a mode of inspiration and a kind of literary production that are not settled, and which fit the evidence of the Scriptures themselves poorly.

*Defending Inerrancy* goes on to say that inerrancy was taught by Christ and the apostles:

> "Inerrancy was taught by Christ and the apostles in the New Testament. This should be our primary basis for believing it. B.B. Warfield said, 'We believe this doctrine of the plenary inspiration of the Scriptures primarily because it is the doctrine which Christ and his apostles believed, and which they have taught us.' To quote Jesus himself, 'the Scripture cannot be broken' (John 10:35) and 'until heaven and earth pass away not an iota, not a dot, will pass away from the Law until all is accomplished' (Matt 5:18)."[35]

This argument seems somewhat disingenuous to me. In the first place, Warfield says that Jesus taught *inspiration*, not inerrancy as the article defines it. The debate isn't over inspiration—about which we all agree—it's about how we understand truth and error in biblical genres.

Secondly, the texts cited—John 10:35 and Matt 5:18—both indicate that Scripture will certainly *achieve God's purposes* for it. But does either passage insist that any of the genres of Scripture must be *factual* as well as true? Does either passage insist upon historical and scientific accuracy in

---

34. Cf. *Chicago Statement on Biblical Inerrancy*, Article VII.
35. Defending Inerrancy, *What is Biblical Inerrancy?*

any way? In fact, when Jesus says: "Scripture cannot be broken," he is referring to *poetry*: specifically a line in which the psalmist says to his readers: "You are gods." In order to *not break* a poem, it needs to be read according to the *rules of poetry*. Reading it as a list of factual and accurate statements *would* ironically be breaking the Scriptures.

One is able to say that Jesus and the apostles taught *inspiration* of Scripture, but I look in vain for any evidence that they taught inerrancy as it is defined by many evangelicals today.

## The Danger of Putting Inerrancy at the Head of Doctrine

In the introduction to *Five Views on Biblical Inerrancy*, Merrick and Garrett suggest that putting inerrancy at the head of evangelical doctrine can lead to some unintended consequences. One such consequence is that adherents are in danger of viewing doctrines as teachings that are of the same order as facts or scientific theories.

> "Extracting [inerrancy] from its context in the doctrine of revelation and placing it at the head of Christian doctrine can ironically lead to a diminishment of Christian truth . . . [It] seems to teach that Christian beliefs are of the order of facts . . . the Christian is taught that becoming a Christian is about learning the right information rather than submitting to the regeneration of the Holy Spirit."[36]

They point out that this might even *distort* the doctrine of revelation by giving the false impression that we have unmediated, certain access to God's perfect truth, and thus that all other fields of knowledge are merely human, flawed, untrustworthy.

> "A misplaced doctrine of inerrancy leads to overinflated perceptions of our knowledge of truth . . . In modern scientific culture the only ideas that have authority (or rationality) are those rooted in fact . . . The Bible's authority must be understood according to the authority of God and thus should not be reduced to the authority of fact."[37]

If the doctrine of inerrancy is put at the head of doctrine, it has the effect of subjecting hermeneutics (interpretation) to its philosophical view of the

---

36. Merrick and Garrett, "Introduction," 14.
37. Merrick and Garrett, "Introduction," 15–16.

Bible, and so deciding in advance that the Bible cannot present history in certain ways. The Bible must be interpreted in ways that fit their doctrine.

However, hermeneutics should come first. Involved in hermeneutics is the discussion of what the Bible is, what genres it uses, and how literature, history and truth interact. Only once we have answered these questions can we decide whether and in what way texts are inerrant.

## Problems with Inerrancy

The doctrine of inerrancy is always practiced with qualifiers—such as that terms like "sunrise" that reflect human experience don't need to be scientifically factual. However, the longer this list of caveats grows, the hollower it becomes to insist that the Bible is *factually* flawless.

### *The Problem of Errant Editors*

The idea that the doctrine of inerrancy applies only to the autographs (i.e., the original documents)—but not to the work of editors who intentionally or unintentionally corrupted the text—has problems. This suggestion works well enough for New Testament texts, because each book seems to have had a single author who completed a manuscript, and this manuscript was then taken and copied and distributed around the ancient world. However, it is far more difficult to see how this idea of autographs applies to many or most of the Old Testament texts.

Consider the Torah and the Former Prophets (Genesis to 2 Kings). The story in these books begins in the periods that played host to Adam and Abraham and ends with Israel exiled by Assyria and Babylon—a period of perhaps fifteen-hundred years. Yet each of these books picks up seamlessly from where the previous one left off. This suggests either that each book was canonized early and in sequence, and later authors therefore knew to resume the previous story, or it suggests that the books were edited together at a later time. A number of clues in the texts suggest that a writer or editor is looking at these stories from a distance, which might suggest the latter of these two options. Here are a few examples:

> "When Abram heard that his kinsman had been taken captive, he led forth his trained men, born in his house, 318 of them, and went in pursuit *as far as Dan.*" (Gen 14:14)

The narrator of this part of Genesis uses the place-name Dan in reference to (most likely) the far north of the Promised Land. Dan was allocated its location in the heart of Israel in the book of Joshua, but they moved to the far north in the book of Judges. It could be that Dan was an old Canaanite place name now lost to us, but the texts below also suggest a later perspective and make this quite unlikely. More probably, this implies readership from the time of Joshua or Judges at the earliest.

> "So Abraham called the name of that place, 'The LORD will provide'; as it is said *to this day*, 'On the mount of the LORD it shall be provided.'" (Gen 22:14)

There are many texts in Genesis that use the phrase "to this day" in order to explain some phenomenon that is known to later readers. This example—given Abraham's location in the land of Moriah, seemingly identified by 2 Chr 3:1 as the temple site in Jerusalem—seems to imply that the readers would understand the mount of the Lord to be the *temple mount*. This places them beyond David's time.

> "And Joshua the son of Nun was full of the spirit of wisdom, for Moses had laid his hands on him. So the people of Israel obeyed him and did as the LORD had commanded Moses. *And there has not arisen a prophet since* in Israel like Moses, whom the LORD knew face to face." (Deut 34:9–10)

This text in Deuteronomy seems to imply that the readers have experienced a succession of prophets since the time of Moses and Joshua, none of whom were the match of Moses.

> "And Joshua set up twelve stones in the midst of the Jordan, in the place where the feet of the priests bearing the ark of the covenant had stood; and they are there *to this day*." (Josh 4:9)

> "Yet the people of Israel did not drive out the Geshurites or the Maacathites, but Geshur and Maacath dwell in the midst of Israel *to this day*." (Josh 13:13)

Joshua also implies readers from some time beyond the events of the book itself. Interestingly 13:13 seems to reflect a time before the exile in which Israel is still living in the land. This is particularly significant because the implied time period of the narrator seems not to be consistently from one era. Josh 13:13 seems to be before the exile, but Judg 18:30 seems to be aware of a time *after* the exile:

> "And the people of Dan set up the carved image for themselves, and Jonathan the son of Gershom, son of Moses, and his sons were priests to the tribe of the Danites *until the day of the captivity of the land.*" (Judg 18:30)

Reference to the captivity of the land is uniformly reserved for the exile of Israel and Judah (North: 2 Kgs 15–18; South: 2 Kgs 24–25). It is used in 1 Sam 4 in reference to the exile of God's Ark in Philistia,[38] but it is used of no other Israelite conflict. Geisler and Howe,[39] in an effort to argue that the book of Judges was written in and around the period of the judges, argue that there must have been a captivity of the tribe of Dan shortly after their move—but this is an alleged captivity that is not known to us from history or the Bible. Given that reference to the "captivity of the land" elsewhere in Scripture is consistently a reference to the exiles of Israel and Judah, without actual evidence to the contrary it seems more likely that readers of this edition of Judges knew about the exiles too.

In short, the evidence suggests that the Old Testament narratives contain stories that were very old, and perhaps from various oral and written sources, but that were collected and/or edited much later. There may even have been more than one edition from different editors at different times before the books reached their final form.

This is a problem for the mechanics of inerrancy and its application to the autographs, because a number of Old Testament books seem to have reached their final form through a process that is the reverse of that in the New Testament. It seems highly probable that they didn't have a single autographic author, but were compiled and changed over time. So the original stories that make up, say, Genesis are technically not the inspired ones. It is the editor's compilation, structuring, and narration within them—all of which is essential to the theological meaning of the stories—that produced the inspired edition.

Of course God is free to inspire whomever, whatever, and whenever he sees fit, but the usual explanation that relies on inerrancy of the inspired author's autographs and not the editors only applies to the New Testament. It's an argument that shouldn't be overplayed.

---

38. Even this is consistent—it is a foreshadowing of the exiles that end Samuel-Kings.
39. Geisler and Howe, *Judges 18:30*.

## Some Examples of Conflicts with Fact

Defenders of rigid inerrancy have done the church a great service in their attempts to resolve apparent contradictions in the Bible. There are many passages that seem to offer insurmountable challenges to the truth of the Scriptures, and yet many of these problems are due to our own misunderstandings or can be resolved when they are looked at in the right way. It would be easy for us to merely throw up our arms and resign ourselves to the challenges that come from critical scholarship or opponents of Christianity. Without those who have carefully applied their minds to what Scripture means and how it communicates, it could easily seem as though the Bible is an irredeemable mess of contradictions. I would urge none of us to surrender our convictions too lightly.

Nevertheless, we can only interpret the Bible clearly and resolve difficulties by *genuinely* understanding how Scripture means to communicate, and by ridding ourselves of prejudices and presumptions that have introduced conflicts that aren't really there. If, for example, we find that some Scriptures that we had assumed to be merely factual are actually trying to communicate by other means, it might force us to modify our doctrine, but it will nevertheless be *progress* towards truth, not a departure from it.

The few examples that follow are some of those that are hard to reconcile with complete factuality.

### Length of the Judges Era

In Judg 2:11–19, the narrator supplies us with a general pattern of rebellion and salvation that occurred under the rule of the judges, which it then traces for each of the six main judges that feature in the book. According to this general pattern, the judge would lead the nation back to God, but sometime after the judge's death the nation would rebel and become *more corrupt* than before:

> "Whenever the LORD raised up judges for them, the LORD was with the judge, and he saved them from the hand of their enemies all the days of the judge. For the LORD was moved to pity by their groaning because of those who afflicted and oppressed them. But *whenever the judge died*, they turned back and *were more corrupt than their fathers*, going after other gods, serving them and bowing down to them." (2:18–19a)

This is the pattern that the careers of the judges follow (though with increasing complication as the judges and the nation get worse)—each judge leads their people in victory, there is the announcement of peace at least during the remainder of his or her lifetime, and once they die, the nation is depicted as rebelling again.

The problem with this presentation is that the time periods given in the book add up to more than four-hundred years. To this must be added the forty years of wandering in the wilderness and thirty years of Joshua's leadership that preceded the period of the judges. Conservative calculations of the date of the exodus put it as early as the 1440s BC. If you subtract 470 years from the date of the exodus, it gives us approximately the year 970 BC—probably the latter part of David's rule and far beyond the judges period.

There have been explanations offered for this problem; one suggests that the rules of the judges were only successive when the Bible explicitly says things like "After him," such as in Judg 3:31. All the other times reigns might have overlapped. That is all very well, but the pattern that we're explicitly told is that each judge died and after his death (and sometimes an extended time of peace) another rebellion occurred and another judge was raised. There is no hint in the text itself that anything other than the pattern expressed in chapter 2 is taking place. The idea of overlapping reigns is surely the solution to the chronology problem, but it doesn't seem to me to solve the problem of the facts as the text presents them.

## Elkanah's Heritage

Elkanah was the father of Samuel the prophet, and he is mentioned in both 1 Samuel and 1 Chronicles. The problem is that Elkanah is introduced in 1 Sam 1 in this way:

> "There was a certain man of Ramathaim-zophim of the hill country of Ephraim whose name was Elkanah."

However, in 1 Chr 6:16–23, Elkanah is in the line of *Levi*.

Geisler and Howe propose as a solution that *both* of these genealogies are correct. Because Eli the priest took Samuel into service at the tabernacle, it makes sense that he needed to be of the tribe of Levi. In terms of the lineage in 1 Samuel, they say:

> "The statement in 1 Samuel 1:1 simply points out that Elkanah lived in the mountains of Ephraim. All the Levites were assigned to dwell in certain cities that were scattered throughout the tribes of Israel... Elkanah was a Levite by tribal descent and an Ephraimite by geographical location."[40]

While their explanation is quite right, they have left out the more puzzling part of the 1 Samuel text. The full verse reads:

> "There was a certain man of Ramathaim-zophim of the hill country of Ephraim whose name was Elkanah the son of Jeroham, son of Elihu, son of Tohu, son of Zuph, *an Ephrathite*." (1 Sam 1:1)

Geisler and Howe have explained how Elkanah can be a Levite living in Ephraim, but they have not explained how he can be both a Levite and an "Ephrathite." There is some discussion over whether this refers to an Ephrathite from Bethlehem in Judah[41] or to an Ephraimite.[42] Either way, it seems highly likely that "Ephrathite" designates Elkanah's tribal affiliation.[43] Whether he is a Judahite or an Ephraimite living in the hills of Ephraim, Elkanah in 1 Samuel 1:1 seems not to be a Levite.

### God's Verdict on David

In 1 Kgs 14:8, God sends a message via his prophet to the rebellious king Jeroboam. God says:

> "[I] tore the kingdom away from the house of David and gave it to you, and yet you have not been like my servant David, who kept my commandments and followed me with all his heart, doing only that which was right in my eyes."

If the telling of history must be accurate and factual in every statement, how can God say that David did only what was right in his eyes? One chapter later, also apparently presenting us with perfectly accurate and factual statements, we read:

---

40. Geisler and Howe, *1 Samuel 1:1*.
41. See Gen 35:19 and 1 Sam 17:12.
42. It seems as though "Ephraimite" is occasionally spelled identically to "Ephrathite." See Judg 12:5 and 1 Kgs 11:26.
43. It is customary to identify someone by tribe (see 1 Sam 9:1 and 17:12) but this information for Samuel himself is given nowhere else in the book.

"because David did what was right in the eyes of the LORD and did not turn aside from anything that he commanded him all the days of his life, except in the matter of Uriah the Hittite." (1 Kgs 15:5)

Both these things cannot be *factually* true at the same time. If the truth of biblical history depends on factuality, then 1 Kgs 14:8 is a lie. If you protest that "we all know what God is getting at" or "this is just a way of speaking," then you are correct. But you cannot have it both ways. Either inerrant Scriptures must be factual (in which case this is an error), or inerrant Scriptures *subordinate factuality* to the rules of the kind of text in question. God is able to say something factually false, but it nevertheless remains *true* because the purpose is to make a general contrast between David and Jeroboam, not to give a full, factual account of David's transgressions.

## Matthew's Genealogy

Matthew's genealogy of Jesus is puzzling in several ways. The names that Matthew lists are as follows:

| Abraham to David | David to Exile | Exile to Jesus |
|---|---|---|
| Abraham | Solomon | (Jechoniah) |
| Isaac | Rehoboam | Shealtiel |
| Jacob | Abijah | Zerubbabel |
| Judah | Asaph | Abiud |
| Perez | Jehoshaphat | Eliakim |
| Hezron | Joram | Azor |
| Ram | Uzziah | Zadok |
| Amminadab | Jotham | Achim |
| Nahshon | Ahaz | Eliud |
| Salmon | Hezekiah | Eleazar |
| Boaz | Manasseh | Matthan |
| Obed | Amos | Jacob |
| Jesse | Josiah | Joseph |
| David | Jechoniah | Jesus |

The first problem is that the third list of names does not add up to fourteen—there are only thirteen. The obvious solution is that Jeconiah should end the second list *and* begin the third:

> "Jeconiah is counted in both lists, since he lived both before and after the captivity. So, there are literally 14 names listed 'from the captivity in Babylon until the Christ,' just as Matthew says. There are also literally 14 names listed between David and the captivity, just as Matthew claims . . . There is no error in the text at all."[44]

This explanation would seem to save Matthew from miscounting, but there are some problems for proponents of strict factuality. To say "there are literally 14 names listed . . . just as Matthew says" is a little misleading, because that is *not* what Matthew says. Matthew says there were fourteen *generations*, not fourteen names. Jeconiah's life may have bridged the deportation, but it is not *factually* accurate to count him twice when numbering generations.

Even if we were to accept that it's appropriate to count the number of *names*, it creates another problem. The presentation of the names is consistent in ending one list and beginning the next with the same name. Just as Jeconiah's name begins the third list, David's name is repeated at the head of the second list, and this yields a count of fifteen names, not fourteen.

A more serious problem with the list, in my opinion, is that Matthew's second list says that "Joram begot Uzziah," whereas the story in Kings and the genealogy in 1 Chr 3:11–12 both confirm that between Joram and Uzziah were *three more generations*: Ahaziah, Joash, and Amaziah.

The solution given by Geisler and Howe is that genealogies use the words "son" and "father" loosely:

> "'Begot' means 'became the ancestor of,' and the one 'begotten' is the 'descendant of.' Matthew, therefore, is not giving a complete chronology, but an abbreviated genealogy of Christ's ancestry."[45]

This accounts well for problems with genealogies in general—if the convention is to list *a* descendant and not necessarily the *immediate* descendant, then that's just how the genre works.

The problem in this case is that Matthew's genealogy is unique. He is not merely listing members of a family line; he is also making a point about *how many* descendants there were between major markers in Israel's history. A factual, plain reading of the text should not allow there to be seventeen generations when only fourteen were claimed.

---

44. Geisler and Howe, *Matthew 1:17*.
45. Geisler and Howe, *Matthew 1:8*.

One technique of harmonization might be tempting at this point—it is often argued that a higher number in one text necessarily includes the lower number. For example, in Mark 5:2 Jesus meets a demon-possessed man named Legion, but in the parallel story in Matthew, he claims that there were *two* demon-possessed men (8:28). This isn't a problem, because Mark doesn't *have to* mention the full number. If there were two men, then it is also true that there was one. He's free to restrict his interest to some details and not others.

There comes a point, however, at which harmonizations of this sort begin to strain credulity. Robert Gundry raises such an issue with the attempted harmonization of the details of Jesus' crucifixion. Harold Lindsell had argued that disagreement in the Gospels meant that Peter must have denied Jesus *six times* rather than only three. Gundry says:

> "During a telephone conversation long ago, I told Lindsell, 'Harold, the Bible says that Peter denied Jesus three times, not six.' He answered, 'Well, if Peter denied Jesus six times, he must have denied him three times.' Which answer harms rather than helps the view of Scripture held by biblicists."[46]

This sort of harmonization works in certain circumstances, but it is surely unacceptable from the perspective of rigid inerrancy to claim that if there were actually seventeen generations between David and the exile, then there were also fourteen. *All* views of inerrancy say that the Bible does not mislead us, and yet if Matthew's point is to show symmetry in God's plan by pointing to three lists of fourteen generations, how is it anything but misleading (in terms of factual accuracy) if that symmetry is artificial?

Furthermore, by the same reasoning, there were also *four* generations between Abraham, David, the exile, and Jesus. Or two. Does this sort of presentation have any relationship to fact and truth if the author is able to claim any number as long as it is not higher than the actual number? Matthew's statement about the number of generations would be factual only on a technicality—one that is a violation of plain reading—and I don't see how it can be argued that it is accurate.

In short, it is possible to rescue the factuality of Matthew's genealogy, but only at the cost of its truth. One either allows that Matthew's count of fourteen is not intended to be historically accurate—perhaps because it was chosen for theological purposes (e.g., by blotting out ill-favored generations

---

46. Gundry, *Smithereens!*

from Jesus' line altogether or because there is symbolic significance to the number)—or one would surely have to accuse him of willfully misleading his reader.

## Playing Russian Roulette with the Gospel

Satisfactory solutions to such difficulties that can rescue the full factuality of the Bible may exist or later emerge. Whether they do or not, the more crucial point is that Geisler and other proponents of a rigid, factual inerrancy are effectively *wagering the evangelical faith* on there never being a biblical statement that can be proven to be inaccurate.

### *The Wager in the Chicago Statements*

The *Chicago Statement on Biblical Inerrancy* lays out the necessity of inerrancy as a doctrine and, depending on how certain things are defined, it is helpful enough. The other Chicago Statement—concerning hermeneutics—is less helpful, particularly because it most clearly lays down a wager that seems to me to gamble the car keys and the deeds to the family house.

Consider the following articles:

> "Article XX. WE AFFIRM that since God is the author of all truth, all truths, biblical and extrabiblical, are consistent and cohere, and that the Bible speaks truth when it touches on matters pertaining to nature, history, or anything else. We further affirm that in some cases extrabiblical data have value for clarifying what Scripture teaches, and for prompting correction of faulty interpretations. WE DENY that extrabiblical views ever disprove the teaching of Scripture or hold priority over it."

> "Article XXI. WE AFFIRM the harmony of special with general revelation and therefore of biblical teaching with the facts of nature. WE DENY that any genuine scientific facts are inconsistent with the true meaning of any passage of Scripture."

> "Article XXII. WE AFFIRM that Genesis 1–11 is factual, as is the rest of the book. WE DENY that the teachings of Genesis 1–11 are mythical and that scientific hypotheses about earth history or the origin of humanity may be invoked to overthrow what Scripture teaches about creation."

Articles XX and XXI both affirm that all truth is God's truth, and so both articles agree that biblical knowledge and that of the sciences should *cohere*. Article XX goes the step further to say that extrabiblical information is even able to *correct our interpretations* should we be shown to have erred in our reading of Scripture. These are both good and necessary points to underline.

However, in spite of these affirmations, Article XXII proceeds to contradict these helpful concessions just made to general revelation. Follow the train of thought in these articles:

- Article XX denies that information outside the Bible is able to correct something that *the Bible* says. In other words, there is a difference between Scripture and *our interpretation* of Scripture. The latter can be corrected; the former cannot.
- Article XXI claims that *genuine* scientific fact and *true* interpretation will never be in conflict. In other words, if there is a conflict, it is either our interpretation of the word or the scientist's interpretation of the world that is at fault.
- Article XXII declares that Gen 1–11 is *fact* and scientific hypotheses cannot correct what the Bible teaches about creation.

The problem here is that the description of Gen 1–11 as *fact* is a statement about its *genre*. The authors are declaring what kind of literature they think they're reading—it is factual, not mythical (or anything else). However, texts do not usually announce their genres, which is why scholars disagree as to what genre we ought to ascribe to texts such as Gen 1–11. A decision about the genre of a text is a matter of *human interpretation*, which means, according to Article XX, that extrabiblical information should be able to help correct our genre mistakes, even in Genesis. However, Article XXII in effect *denies that it is possible* that they might have erred on this point. Scientific hypotheses are not allowed to challenge their teaching that Gen 1–11 is fact after all.

The articles weigh in on the matter of genre in this way:

> "Article XIII. WE AFFIRM that awareness of the literary categories, formal and stylistic, of the various parts of Scripture is essential for proper exegesis, and hence we value genre criticism as one of the many disciplines of biblical study."

This article implies that applying the incorrect genre rules to a text would amount to misinterpretation—something with which I wholeheartedly agree. To call Gen 1–11 *fact* is to assign it a literary category—a set of genre rules. The article acknowledges that if these have been incorrectly applied, it would mean that the interpreter has missed a key component of proper exegesis of the text and is teaching falsely.

However, the denial part of the same article reads as follows:

> "WE DENY that generic categories which negate historicity may rightly be imposed on biblical narratives which present themselves as factual."

After just affirming that we *must* let the Bible's genres speak in their own way for fear of misinterpretation, the article proceeds to deny that certain genres are allowed to be applied to biblical narratives, because they present themselves as factual. But do they? *How* do they present themselves as factual? There are many genres that represent the past, such as poetry, storytelling, and even myth, none of which are what we classify as history, and each has a different relationship to fact. The question is: what sort of past-related literature is Genesis or Exodus? We describe these books as history and read with our expectations of historical literature, but what expectations did ancient readers have of this kind of history-writing? What was the relationship of *their* histories to fact?

In continuity with Geisler's view that Matthew ought to have seen himself as "reporting events" in his Gospel, Article VI says:

> "Article VI. . . . We further affirm that a statement is true if it *represents matters as they actually are*, but is an error if it *misrepresents the facts*."

This statement again seems to me to imply that truthful writing about the past must exist to tell us "what happened." Because biblical texts write about the past, they must therefore be this sort of history. However, there are some apparent differences between the modernist genre of history that this article seems to assume and the genre of history in the biblical narratives: modernist history tries to objectively record *facts and events*, whereas the biblical stories are *narrative* history and the focus is on *characters* and *conversations* and *God's perspective* on the past—perhaps like a screenplay would tell history.

Modernist history (reportage) focused on events because they are the most objective things to report on—they are observable and can be gleaned from eye-witness reports. Modernist history avoided things that the biblical narratives revel in—dialogues (because they are not recorded or remembered well), judgements and verdicts (because they betray bias), and artistic wordplay, repetitions, symbols, etc. (because they are emotive and don't lend themselves to reportage).

In summary, the idea that biblical stories "present themselves as factual" and ought to be reporting events is based on an assumed philosophy of history-writing, not on the biblical histories as we have them. The biblical narratives don't *present themselves* as factual. That's not how genre analysis works—genres rarely declare themselves; they just assume the reader will be familiar enough with the rules to eventually catch on. This is not to say that none of them *are* factual, but merely that none of them explicitly present themselves as such.

The book of Job begins with typical biblical narration—identifying people and places and so on—but the narrator of the Job story is omniscient. He is able to observe conversations between God and the Accuser in heaven, and he is able to give background information that was never disclosed to Job or seemingly anyone else. Omniscient narrators are not a feature of reportage, but they are common in biblical narrative.

Likewise, the book of Jonah is typical narrative and it stars a real prophet. On its own, Jonah reads like a fable or an extended parable. He lives for three days in a fish. Foreigners in the book (such as the sailors and the Ninevites) are quick to honor God, whereas Jonah consistently cares only about himself. Jonah is angry that God grants Nineveh repentance and angry that God gives him shade only to take it away again. The book appears to be a contrast between the merciful God and the entitled, grumbling, uncaring Israelites. Is there anything about the form of the book or its terminology that declares it to be factual?[47] How would it differ in form if it were intended to be read as a parable?

The whole point of genre study is to determine what kinds of narrative we have in the Bible, what its general rules are, and what this implies of its connection to fact and history. If correct genre analysis is essential to proper exegesis, as the statements say, then such analysis is a matter of

---

47. Again, to be clear, I am not saying that Job or Jonah are definitely *not* factual; I am only pointing out that nothing about their presentation allows us to say with certainty that these books are or are not factual. They are *true* and, if based on real events, are *true reflections of history*, but they are not for that reason *factual* representations of history. Genre is far more complicated than that.

fallible human interpretation, and a matter that stands prior to determining to what degree a text means to be understood as fact.

To declare on the *factuality* of a text such as Genesis is to *assign it a genre*, and to insist that nothing may challenge the factual historicity of a narrative is to decide in advance that one's analysis is unimpeachable—in violation of the affirmations of Article XIII and Article XX. Declaring that Genesis is fact is an attempt to end the discussion on evolution, but it risks enshrining misinterpretation in an article of faith.

*What Evangelicalism Stands to Lose*

Why is all of this important? The Chicago Statements continue to wield widespread influence over evangelical churches, particularly in America, and yet they describe an approach to Scripture that is worryingly risky.

The "Russian roulette" problem is this. What if the proponents of rigid inerrancy and their Chicago Statements are wrong, and someone were to prove without doubt that a certain text in, say, Genesis is not factual? You may say that this will never happen, but what if it did?

Creationist organizations have been teaching for decades that Jesus was a creationist and the gospel depends on creationism being true. If, say, the Genesis creation story reuses ancient Near Eastern myths and isn't aiming at fact, what should happen to their evangelical faith? By their definitions, the word of God would therefore be *lying*. To reiterate, I am not asking what would happen if we found out that the Bible were *untrue*; I am merely asking what would happen if biblical narratives were shown beyond question to be of a genre that *isn't* primarily factual (but might be true on other grounds). Is evangelicalism *over*? Is *Christianity* over? If we have a lying Bible, it should be.

While those insisting on factuality in the Bible's narratives ought to deconvert if such evidence emerged, in practice, I suspect that most would merely adapt their beliefs to a view of narrative that is more flexible.

Such adaptation of belief has already taken place many times before. For example, Seely[48] points out that human cultures on every continent have recorded belief in the idea of a "firmament"—that is, a solid dome that literally meets the earth at the horizon and that could be touched if one were able to travel there. This was also the Hebrew belief (Gen 1:8, Ezek 1:22–28) and it persisted through Western history at least until the

48. Seely, "Firmament," 229–36.

Renaissance. When it was conclusively proven not to be the case, biblical interpretation adjusted accordingly. B. B. Warfield's conclusion was that biblical authors could write inerrantly while still reflecting the ordinary (mistaken) opinions of their day on peripheral matters.[49] But such an option is not available to us if we insist on strict, factual inerrancy.

Unfortunately, for many people today, the threshold of proof that the Bible is not fully factual has already been reached, and the attempts of rigid inerrantists to explain the objections away have not persuaded them. You can accuse them of lack of faith if you want, but those who have only known church traditions that affirm and deny their way out of Bible difficulties find no help there in reconciling God's word and God's world. Those traditions that use fear (of liberals or evolutionists or a slippery slope to moral bankruptcy) to compel obedience to their doctrines force such people to comply or depart, and many are choosing to depart.

## Conclusion

Inerrancy has historically referred to the belief in the truthfulness of Scripture, and not to a particular statement about what genres God was allowed to inspire the writers of Scripture to use. I affirm with the Chicago Statements that it is essential for proper exegesis that we do *not* assume the genre of a text, but analyze the literary forms that we have in Scripture and interpret its content appropriately to the genres that it uses.

If this means that we must accept that the authors of Scripture used genres to write about the past that conformed to the standards and expectations *of the ancient world*—hardly a controversial idea—and that they were unfamiliar with an approach to history that insisted upon fact as the primary criterion of truth, then so be it. To repeat—it is *essential to exegesis* that we do so, even if we find that the genre employs creativity where we would have preferred fact and certainty.

It *might just be*, for example, that the Genesis account of creation uses elements of other creation stories familiar in the ancient world in order to correct the distortions of ancient worldviews with true theology. It *might just be* that is does not intend to give modern people an easy answer to the problem of evolution. What of it? It is not for us to decide what sort of information the Bible is allowed to provide. That was God's decision.

---

49. Seely, "Firmament," 240.

There are many evangelicals whose studies of ancient literature have caused them to believe that biblical genres do not conform to our preferred standards of history-writing. They argue that the way in which stories about the past were told made allowances for "narrative license," much as we still make allowances for "poetic license." In other words, if the biblical genres of history-writing are less concerned with careful adherence to factual details, but, like poetry, are more concerned with communicating the theological significance of the past for the reader's present, then divergences from pure fact are not errors.

It is natural to us to allow that poetry may take license with fact and to allow that it may represent the past creatively without needing to accuse the poet of lying. It is natural to us because *our* expectations of poetry and *ancient* expectations of poetry are similar in this regard. It is unnatural for us to allow that ancient historians might have had a creative role in their representations of the past because we assume that we are reading history, not story or prophecy, and that history must be written a certain way. There is, in fact, no reason why people in the ancient world shouldn't have had similar expectations of creativity and factuality in their poetry *and* their narrative. Our strong distinction between the two is a modern preoccupation and an artificial one.

One of my favorite books is called *The Curious Incident of the Dog in the Night-Time* by Mark Haddon. The book is written from the perspective of a boy called Christopher who has an unspecified developmental disorder, seemingly on the autism spectrum. One of the things that this boy is unable to cope with is lies, which he views as a personal betrayal. At one point he discusses the different relationship of metaphor and simile to truth and lies:

> "The word *metaphor* means carrying something from one place to another, and it comes from the Greek words μετα (which means *from one place to another*) and φερειν (which means *to carry*), and it is when you describe something by using a word for something that it isn't. This means that the word *metaphor* is a metaphor. I think it should be called a lie because a pig is not like a day[50] and people do not have skeletons in their cupboards. And when I try to make a picture of the phrase in my head it just confuses me because imagining an apple in someone's eye doesn't have anything to do with liking someone a lot and it makes you forget what the person was talking about."[51]

50. Referring to the metaphor: "We had a real pig of a day."
51. Haddon, *Curious Incident*, 15.

When describing a policeman, he says "It looked as if there were two very small mice hiding in his nostrils," and he adds:

> "This is not a *metaphor*, it is a *simile*, which means that it really did look like there were two very small mice hiding in his nostrils, and if you make a picture in your head of a man with two very small mice in his nostrils, you will know what the police inspector looked like. And a simile is not a lie, unless it is a bad simile."[52]

I quote this at length, because I think it is a parable for our own inconsistency in terms of interpreting the relationship of poetry and narrative to truth and fact, and it also introduces an excellent example of non-factual information in historical material that is nevertheless true: *metaphor*. It is uncontested that all language is replete with the use of metaphor and that biblical narratives are no exception. However, as Christopher points out, in their relationship to fact, metaphors are *lies* because they claim that something is what it is not. Nevertheless, none of us attempts to explain away the seeming factual error of metaphors in the Bible (such as trying to explain how Jacob's son Judah might have really been part lion-cub [Gen 49:9]), because it is a convention in both poetry and narrative that we readily accept as true though it isn't factual.

This passage is humorous because we can appreciate that Christopher is technically correct but only because he is force-fitting something into his way of seeing the world that doesn't belong there. In a similar way, the insistence from some quarters that biblical histories must be literal might well be because they're attempting to force-fit the Bible into conventions that make sense to them, but that might not have made nearly as much sense to the Bible's authors.

In summary, we have enough examples in our own genres of literature of ways in which historical information might be presented using devices and genres that depart from fact but nevertheless communicate truth. A text can remain *inerrant* though it is poetry or metaphor or parable or myth or fiction, because genres have different purposes and they have different relationships to history and fact. If they communicate truth in accordance with the purposes and techniques inherent to their genre, they do not *err* though they aren't factual or historical (in the modernist sense of the word).

I say with the early J. I. Packer that evangelicalism demands that we are sensitive to the literary character of texts. It does not demand a *literalistic*

---

52. Haddon, *Curious Incident*, 17.

approach to texts. No text *presents itself as factual*. Every text has a relationship to fact and history, but it is not our place to decide in advance—or based on our preferences—what that relationship must be.

# Chapter 4

# What the Bible Seems To Be

*The secret things belong to the LORD our God, but the things that are revealed belong to us and to our children forever . . . (Deut 29:29)*

It seems obvious to say that our beliefs about the Bible can't be determined by what we think the Bible *ought to be*. Our beliefs must be based upon what the Bible says about itself and upon observation of what kinds of literature we find in it—what the Bible *seems to be*.

In the previous chapter, we mentioned briefly some of the texts in Scripture that reflect upon the nature of God's word and which can be suitably applied to the Bible as a whole. Chiefly, it is clear that the Bible is inspired by God, that it was written—generally speaking—by ordinary human means, and that it is wholly true. We discussed at length some of the beliefs that Christians have extrapolated out from these points, and which seem not to fit the evidence of Scripture itself—the inspiration of the Bible does not seem to have resulted in omniscience on the part of the authors, it has not resulted in clarity in interpretation, and its truth and historicity does not mean that it only reports events or speaks factually.

So, what conclusions about the nature of Scripture should we as readers infer from what we find in its pages?

## Scripture is Indeterminate

Christians are familiar with difference of opinion when it comes to the interpretation and application of Scripture. While the easiest solution is to assume that the other team is in error, the problem does not always resolve itself that easily.

R. T. France[1] examined more carefully the issue of women in the church's ministry as an example of Christians following the same sufficient and perspicuous Scriptures and yet reaching *opposite conclusions* about such important matters. His study ably demonstrates that complementarianism and egalitarianism can *both* claim to be the product of responsible exegesis of biblical evidence; each position merely prioritizes and applies texts differently.

Even within traditions and sub-traditions there is not uniformity of interpretation. Hübner,[2] for example, claims to have identified *eight* different interpretations of 1 Tim 2:12—just by complementarians. So although we might all similarly commit to inspired and infallible Scriptures, and even though we might belong to the same school of thought on a subject, we nevertheless do not always come to the same conclusions about what a text means or how it ought to be applied.

In the previous chapter, I argued these sorts of disagreements make it hard to argue that Scripture is always *clear*. On the contrary, when we look at the kinds of literature that we have in Scripture, a more appropriate model for Scripture than clarity is *indeterminacy*.

## Indeterminacy

According to the *Oxford Dictionary*, something is indeterminate when it is "not exactly known, established, or defined." This might seem an alien concept to apply to the Bible, but consider the following features of the Bible as we have it:

### Narrative and Minimal Explanation

The first half of both Old and New Testaments are written in the narrative genre. We are so accustomed to this fact that it is something that we do not

---

1. France, *Women*, 14.
2. Hübner, *Adventures*, 14:30.

question, but it is nevertheless a strange choice. The Torah, for example, has as one of its major roles the giving of Israel's law, yet this is done through the medium of story. *Our* law books tend to be long, detailed, and matter-of-fact. They do not typically tell the story of how they were given or depict characters trying to live out the laws in the more complicated realm of real life. Israel's law is surprisingly short and covers surprisingly little—most counts identify just over six hundred laws—but the people are called to inhabit the spirit of the law, to write it on their hearts, and thus to shape their behavior by the principles it teaches. As Paul argues, not muzzling one's ox was not *only* about oxen; it invited Israel to explore ways in which that ethic might apply elsewhere. Similarly, the Gospels in the New Testament provide four accounts of Jesus' life, death, and resurrection, all of which exhibit similarities and differences that are notoriously difficult to harmonize.

If we set out to write a religion, and if we wished to give people clear truths about God, the path to knowing him, and the way we ought to live, what sort of material would we have written? In the first place, it would have been better to have one Gospel, written by Jesus himself—perhaps like a new book of Deuteronomy—after his resurrection in which he laid out the implications of his life and death and gave us instructions for how to live. Many of the books would read more like a systematic theology—they would lay out all the essential concepts and when it commanded us to, say, baptize, it would tell us what baptism means and what it is for.

It is strange that when God wrote the book of the Christian faith, he preserved no writings of Jesus himself, he gave us four accounts pieced together from various sources that aren't in perfect agreement, and they are in story form. None of this is calculated to produce *clarity*.

## The Nature of the Hebrew Language and Storytelling

The way in which these stories are communicated only adds to the distance removed from clarity and simplicity. The preferences of Hebrew thought seem to *enjoy* indeterminacy rather than fixity.

As an undergraduate student, I opted not to proceed with Hebrew studies because I reasoned that I would never surpass the language skill of Bible translators, so I might as well rely on the English text (and I would probably spend most of my time in the New Testament anyway).[3] What I didn't realize at the time was that English translations of Hebrew often

---

3. The joke was on me; I eventually became an Old Testament lecturer.

don't merely convert one language into another, but they also convert the Hebrew way of thinking about communication into the English way of thinking about it.

In contrast to my confidence in our translators, Robert Alter, in an essay provocatively titled *The Bible in English and the Heresy of Explanation*, complains:

> "Modern English versions—especially in their treatment of Hebrew narrative prose—have placed readers at a grotesque distance from the distinctive literary experience of the Bible in its original language."[4]

The reason for this, he explains, is that the English preference for written communication is to prize clarity—so we use diverse vocabulary in order to find the precise word, and we use a variety of conjunctions to carefully express the connections between sentences. To the English ear, too much repetition indicates imprecision and clumsiness. So, translators have tended to try to express the ideas found in the Hebrew in harmony with these English preferences. Alter says:

> "The unacknowledged heresy underlying most modern English versions of the Bible is the use of translation as a vehicle for *explaining* the Bible instead of representing it in another language, and in the most egregious instances this amounts to explaining away the Bible. This impulse may be attributed . . . to a feeling that the Bible, because of its canonical status, has to be made accessible—indeed, transparent—to all."[5]

In contrast to the English love of clarity, Hebrew literature tends to prefer non-specific conjunctions (the majority of sentences are joined with an "and"), playful repetition of key words, and intentional ambiguities or unexplained juxtapositions. Alter says:

> "Literature in general, and the narrative prose of the Hebrew Bible in particular, cultivates certain profound and haunting enigmas, delights in leaving its audience guessing about motives and connections, and, above all, loves to set ambiguities of word choice and image against one another in an endless interplay that resists neat resolution."[6]

---

4. Alter, *Five Books of Moses*, xvii.
5. Alter, *Five Books of Moses*, xix.
6. Alter, *Five Books of Moses*, xviii.

## What the Bible Seems To Be

The result of the Hebrew mode of storytelling is that connections between sentences or concepts are not made explicit, but rather invite the reader to explore possibilities. Tamara Cohn Eskenazi says that the indeterminate nature of Hebrew storytelling was something that ancient Jewish interpreters eagerly took up:

> "The rabbis reveled in multiplicity of meanings and the playfulness of the text... They said the Torah has seventy faces. And the revelation at Sinai had 600,000 different meanings, as many as the persons who heard it."[7]

The indeterminacy of Hebrew storytelling is not limited to the Old Testament. The Gospels all show some of the same tendencies to delight in wordplay, ambiguity, omission, and so on—the Gospel of John perhaps more so than the others. John includes such features as:

- *Double meaning:* In 1:5, the verb might mean that the darkness has not *overcome* the light, or *understood* the light (or both).
- *Allusions:* Jesus refers to Nathanael as an Israelite without deceit in 1:47, which seems to be a veiled contrast to the original man Israel (i.e., Jacob) who was full of deceitful trickery. In the same episode, Jesus also alludes to a new and greater "Jacob's ladder" event.
- *Key words:* Jesus' "hour" in John frequently refers to his death; its use in chapter 2 at the wedding at Cana, along with seeming agitation on his part (2:4), perhaps intends for us to bring his crucifixion to mind. The reasons for this are not made clear in the text.
- *Symbols:* The fact that Nicodemus approaches Jesus *by night* in chapter 3 seems either to show secretiveness on Nicodemus's part or perhaps to associate him with the darkness that would not understand or overcome the light. The recurring motif of water in the early chapters—for baptism, in ceremonial jars, being born of water, taking water from Jacob's well—seems to have symbolic value too, probably most often as representative of the Old Covenant that is being surpassed by baptism in the Spirit, wine at the Messiah's banquet, rebirth in the Spirit, and living water that quenches every thirst.
- *Puzzles:* In John 7, Jesus' brothers goad him to announce his messiahship at the Feast of Tabernacles—the feast in which the king would traditionally have read from the Torah. Jesus claims that he is

---

7. Eskenazi, "Torah as Narrative," 26–27.

not going to the feast, but shortly afterwards he goes anyway. This prompts us to wonder why this inconsistency exists—what is it about his brothers' prompting that caused him to decline? What is it that caused him to go?

All these devices make John's Gospel a rich ground for the mining of its treasures, but they resist neat resolution or lose some of their vitality in the attempt. Certainly the text itself does not make an effort to prevent us from missing important interpretive clues or misunderstanding the point of the text. John 2 allows us to see Jesus apparently being blunt with his mother or enabling the potential overindulgence of the guests by providing large quantities of wine. Chapter 2 ends by saying that Jesus "revealed his glory"—again an idea commonly associated with his *death*—but it does not try to explain what is meant.

Hebrew language conventions and methods of storytelling resist fixed, clear meanings.

### The Use of Showing Rather Than Telling

A further feature of biblical stories is one that many people find perplexing: the narrators of the Bible's stories prefer to *show* their characters in action and offer few explanatory comments or verdicts, rather than *telling* the reader what they ought to think about the events that unfold in their stories.

One interpreter who has found this particularly puzzling is British atheist Richard Dawkins.[8] In his chapter, *The "Good" Book and the Changing Moral Zeitgeist*, Dawkins describes several biblical episodes that tell of horrific behavior perpetrated by their characters.[9] Dawkins claims this as evidence that biblical morality is perverse, but he arrives at this conclusion because of the fact that biblical narrators regularly do not give their readers clarity by labeling behavior as good or bad. Dawkins wrongly assumes that this means that the narrators *approve* of their characters (particularly "heroic" characters such as Abraham or Samson).

One of the examples that he gives—the story of the Levite and the concubine in Judg 19–21—certainly depicts brutality verse after verse.

---

8. Dawkins, *God Delusion*, 268–316.

9. He does also question God's morality, which is a more difficult issue, but the response to Dawkins is similar in either case.

## What the Bible Seems To Be

However, Judges begins with an introduction that explicitly tells us that the book is about Israel's moral downward-spiral (see Judg 2:19), and the entire epilogue (Judg 17–21) is dripping with irony and should most likely be classified as *satire*—a genre in which the storyteller participates in and amplifies the bad behavior that he is critiquing. In other words, Dawkins is making the mistake that religious picketers of movie cinemas often are making—they are insensitive to the subtleties of literary arts in general and irony most particularly. Dawkins's haplessness as an interpreter at least illustrates that the biblical narratives are not at all tooled for clarity or simplicity.

### Possible Use of Story Elements from the Ancient Near East

A final feature of biblical narratives that hint at complexity rather than simple clarity is the apparent use of ancient Near Eastern myths in their telling of Israel's past.

For example, in a Mesopotamian story called the *Atrahasis Epic*, humanity was created to serve the gods because the lesser gods were tired of doing all the work for their superiors. Unfortunately, humanity multiplied so much and became so noisy that they disturbed the sleep of the gods. After failed attempts at curbing human numbers, a flood was sent to put an end to the disturbance. However, Atrahasis was given advance warning and told to build a boat and to fill it with animals and food. The next part of the story is lost, but at the end, the gods regretted destroying their major food source (i.e., sacrifices), and so they allowed humankind to survive.[10]

A second story, called the *Gilgamesh Epic*, also includes an account of a flood intended to undo the creation of humankind. Gilgamesh was a king who allegedly ruled Uruk in Mesopotamia in c.2600 BC. In the story, he meets a man who had survived the flood and been given immortality. One of the gods had favored him and secretly warned him of the gods' plan to destroy the world with a flood. This god commanded him to build a boat on which he could preserve his family and all living creatures from the storm. In this account, the storm ended on the 7th day and dry land emerged on the 12th. To test whether it was safe to leave the boat, the man sent out a

---

10. Van Seters, *Prologue to History*, 47–54.

dove, a swallow, and finally a raven. The third bird did not return, and so all the survivors left the boat and the man sacrificed to the gods in gratitude.[11]

Of course, the similarities to the Noah story are not total—they clearly aren't the *same* story—but it is at least possible that the story in Genesis is reusing these elements in order to make crucial connections of the worldview that lies behind the Mesopotamian versions: the creation was not intended to put humanity in servitude but rather *relationship* with God; the flood was not the result of capriciousness in the heavens but because of human injustice; Noah wasn't saved because one of the gods broke ranks, but because the one God still planned a future with humanity in which the problem of sin could be fully resolved; the sacrifice at the end didn't remind the gods that they needed food, but was a mark of relationship and covenant between God and humanity.[12]

Besides Mesopotamian creation and flood stories that resemble those at the start of Genesis, the Bible also seems to make reference in its poetry to a creation story that *isn't* the one in Genesis. In some Mesopotamian creation myths—particularly *Enuma Elish*—the separation of heaven and earth, and land and sea was the result of a cosmic war in which the chaotic sea goddess Tiamat, represented as a dragon, is slain by Marduk and cut in half. From her divided body he forms the heavens and the earth.

Biblical poetry often mentions Rahab or Leviathan, chaos monsters that God slaughtered in his creative acts:

> "He has inscribed a circle on the face of the waters at the boundary between light and darkness. The pillars of heaven tremble and are astounded at his rebuke. By his power he stilled the sea; by his understanding he shattered Rahab. By his wind the heavens were made fair; his hand pierced the fleeing serpent." (Job 26:10–13)

> "You divided the sea by your might; you broke the heads of the sea monsters on the waters. You crushed the heads of Leviathan; you gave him as food for the creatures of the wilderness. You split open springs and brooks; you dried up ever-flowing streams. Yours is the day, yours also the night; you have established the heavenly lights and the sun. You have fixed all the boundaries of the earth; you have made summer and winter." (Ps 74:13–17)

---

11. Kovacs, *Epic of Gilgamesh*.

12. Of course, it is possible that these stories are similar because they are representations of common memory with the Bible presenting the real facts, but this is unlikely on account of other mythical elements in the Bible that suggests the reuse of story elements common to the time period was appropriate to the narrative genre.

> "O LORD God of hosts, who is mighty as you are, O LORD, with your faithfulness all around you? You rule the raging of the sea; when its waves rise, you still them. You crushed Rahab like a carcass; you scattered your enemies with your mighty arm. The heavens are yours; the earth also is yours; the world and all that is in it, you have founded them." (Ps 89:8–11)
>
> "Awake, awake, put on strength, O arm of the LORD; awake, as in days of old, the generations of long ago. Was it not you who cut Rahab in pieces, who pierced the dragon?" (Isa 51:9)

In these texts, there is clear use of representatives of chaos—a dragon or a serpent that God killed and (in Job and these psalms) thereby divided or stilled the sea. There is regular connection of this defeat of chaos to God's creative acts (the foundation of the world, and setting boundaries for earth, water, light, and darkness).

This apparent use of an alternative creation story borrowed from Mesopotamian myth suggests that Israelite literature (its poetry at least) interacted with the thought world of the day—even its myths.

One final example comes from the book of Exodus. We are familiar with the famous story of Moses being rescued from death as a child by being set adrift in a basket coated with pitch. He is found by an Egyptian princess who names him "Moses" because she "drew him out" of the water.[13] However, there are strong similarities to the story of the Assyrian king Sargon. Here is an excerpt from the Sargon myth:

> "My mother, a high priestess, conceived me, in secret she bore me. She placed me in a reed basket; with bitumen she caulked my hatch. She abandoned me to the river from which I could not escape. The river carried me along: to Aqqi, the water drawer, it brought me. Aqqi, the water drawer, when immersing his bucket lifted me up. Aqqi, the water drawer, raised me as his adopted son. Aqqi, the water drawer, set me to his garden work. During my garden work, Istar loved me (so that) 55 years I ruled as king."[14]

The article from which this extract was taken argues that the similarities are not remarkable enough to require an accounting, there are too many differences between the two, and even if there is dependence, it cannot be

---

13. *Mashah* is the Hebrew word meaning "to draw out"; in Hebrew, "Moses" is actually spelled *Mosheh*. It is interesting that the Sargon story features a water drawer so prominently, though it is possibly a coincidence.

14. Holding, *Sargon vs Moses*.

proved which story depends on which. I don't find these objections persuasive—the whole point of reusing a story would be to signal points of emphasis through the use of *contrasts*. Points of connection to Sargon's story would serve to show how Moses is similar to Sargon, but more especially how he is different from Sargon. We would not expect the two stories to be completely alike.

Whether one is persuaded by these similarities or not, there exists a *prima facie* case for biblical literature borrowing even non-Israelite stories for its own purposes. Either way, if God intended to give us clear Scriptures with accessible interpretation, such confusion could surely have been avoided at the point of their inspiration.

*Poetry, Wisdom, and Paradox*

The third and final draft of Ezra Pound's *In a Station of the Metro* describes a moment of insight that struck him while watching the crowd at a Parisian station. His first draft was thirty lines long, and for about a year he wrestled it down to its essence. In the end, his poem consisted of two verbless lines about apparitions and petals on a black bough.

Whether one finds *In a Station of the Metro* brilliant or a severe anticlimax (I'm edging towards the former), many of us can relate to the feeling that some poetry is too opaque, too inaccessible for its own good. Poetry often operates in the realms of difficult imagery, inner struggle, and multiple meanings.

It is true that not *all* poetry is impenetrable and enigmatic, and much biblical poetry does communicate plainly enough, but it is nevertheless a medium that doesn't aim at clear, propositional truths. For all the contests in modern evangelicalism over the clarity and factuality of Scripture, it is a strange omission from our discussions that *so much* of the Bible's volume is poetry. Psalms, the wisdom literature, and the majority of the prophetic writings come to us in poetic form, which (when totaled up) comes to approximately 45 percent of the total volume of the Old Testament.[15] What does it say about the Bible and God's intentions in revelation that he has elected to communicate with us via a creative, emotive, imagery-laden medium?

---

15. McCulloch, *List of Hebrew Bible Books*. This figure is arrived at by totaling the verse counts of all of Psalms, the wisdom books, and the writing prophets (though only half of Daniel).

## What the Bible Seems To Be

Biblical poetry is valuable for theology despite its creative and emotive nature. Nevertheless it remains a medium that contributes to the indeterminacy of Scripture. It is not always clear how far one should push figurative language or whether it is appropriate to build theology on certain statements. Does the idea that the earth rests on foundations (Ps 104:5) or the heavens on pillars (Job 26:11) have any knowledge value (perhaps as ancient cosmology) or does the speaker intend nothing in terms of its literal correspondence to creation? Does God ride the clouds or not (Ps 104:3)? What does the psalmist mean by calling his readers "gods" (Ps 82:6)?

Biblical poetry regularly makes use of a device called parallelism that pairs lines and implies a relationship between the two. Often within parallelisms or across the whole poem, ideas are put in juxtaposition, a device in which two images are placed side-by-side without any explicit connection being drawn. The effect of this is to offer two snapshots of life. There is intentional lack of explicit connection between the images that it describes—connections that English translations (helpfully? heretically?) tend to supply in order to make the poetry "clear" for us. In Hebrew, however, the images are unresolved, and the reader must explore the reasons for their conjunction.

This doesn't produce interpretive *chaos*—one cannot endlessly multiply interpretations as a result of this technique—but in poetry there is *appreciation* of multiple meanings or ambiguities or relationships that need exploring, and resistance of the impulse to provide clear resolution.

More seriously, biblical poetry leaves far weightier questions largely unresolved. For example, the book of Job spends many, many chapters in discussion of God, the reasons for suffering, and the apportioning of blame—whether to the sufferer or to the God who allows suffering. After all these long poetic monologues in the book, God exonerates Job from blame for his suffering, but nevertheless rebukes him for his lack of understanding and for his distrust of God. As for Job's three friends, God is so against them that they are in danger of severe judgement.

Furthermore, as the book begins to build to a climax, a fourth friend speaks. Elihu angrily silences his elders who have occupied the discussion thus far because, for all their long speeches, they have not come to any answer. He claims that despite his youth, the "breath of the Almighty" (32:8) can enable anyone to reach truth—young or old. He then proceeds to make an argument that seems to me to be virtually indistinguishable from those that came before. In chapter 42, after God has confronted Job, he tells the *three* friends—excluding Elihu—to take an offering to Job and ask him to pray for them so that they can be forgiven.

So what do we make of this? Have the thirty chapters of poetic discussion been incorrect? Can we take nothing from their words except warning, or is some of it true? How do we know what that is? Is Job's friend Elihu different because he is right or because he is so wrong and foolish as to not require serious consideration? Why is he not commended or rebuked or offered forgiveness? Why is he just ignored as though he never spoke?

The individual lines of poetry in Job might be intelligible, but it is an excellent example of indeterminacy all the same. It's too repetitive to preach chapter-by-chapter (but the repetitiveness seems to be central to its point), it "resolves" with about as much mystery as it began, and we can't know whether the vast majority of it is ever useful other than as a cautionary tale.[16]

The entire book of *Song of Songs* is even more perplexing. More like modern poetry, it is frequently enigmatic and dreamlike. It switches speakers so that sometimes it is the woman, sometimes the shepherd, and sometimes still others. It is not clear if this is a poem about God and humanity or love and sex. It is not clear whether the love of the king is a good thing or an act of oppression. Some scholars[17] even see the book as belonging to a genre that intends to "damn with faint praise" and thus to subtly mock Solomon or the sort of power that he represents. The poetry of *Song of Songs* undoubtedly intends to communicate in a deeper and more emotive manner than clear theological statements.

## Wisdom Literature and Paradox

The books that we most clearly associate with wisdom literature (Proverbs and Ecclesiastes) contain lists of aphorisms in poetic form. These books might seem to give us good, clear advice on a variety of topics, but many Christians under-appreciate the degree to which this genre delights in *paradox*. Apparent contradiction is an intentional wisdom device.

---

16. Scholars are similarly divided over Ecclesiastes, with many arguing that the Preacher has lost his way and is a warning to us. See, for example, R. B. Y. Scott's *Anchor Bible Commentary* on Proverbs and Ecclesiastes (1965) and Tremper Longman's *The Book of Ecclesiastes* (1998). Others think that the Preacher communicates genuine godly wisdom.

17. See, for example, Noegel and Rendsburg's *Solomon's Vineyard* (2009).

Consider the following examples:

> "Answer not a fool according to his folly, lest you be like him yourself.
>
> Answer a fool according to his folly, lest he be wise in his own eyes." (Prov 26:4–5)

In successive verses, the writer of these proverbs provides opposite advice: you both should and should not answer a fool.

Consider this section:

> "Disaster pursues sinners,
>
> but the righteous are rewarded with good.
>
> A good man leaves an inheritance to his children's children,
>
> but the sinner's wealth is laid up for the righteous.
>
> The fallow ground of the poor would yield much food,
>
> but it is swept away through injustice.
>
> Whoever spares the rod hates his son,
>
> but he who loves him is diligent to discipline him.
>
> The righteous has enough to satisfy his appetite,
>
> but the belly of the wicked suffers want." (Prov 13:21–25)

In this example, each parallel pair says something about the relationship of prosperity and righteousness. The first and the last pair offer the sort of connection for which Proverbs is best known: the righteous receive blessing but the wicked are cursed for their sin.

However, each intervening pair problematizes this basic principle. There is a sinner who receives *prosperity*, not an empty belly; his curse is merely to be prevented from leaving his wealth as an inheritance. In the central lines, those who appear cursed (the poor) are only so because injustice at the hands of the powerful deprives them of what should rightly be theirs—they are not to blame for their poverty and the *wicked* prosper at their expense. Finally, a son who is greatly loved might nevertheless experience pain and hardship at least for a time, whereas the child who lives without punishment and seemingly in peace is actually without a Father.

Although Proverbs seems to be providing lists of good ideas for successful living, these ideas in combination can introduce conflict and complexity to the picture. Black-and-white principles are rendered increasingly grey. This is because wisdom does not lie in being told *what* to think; it consists in being taught *how* to think. The point is to expose legitimate difficulty in godly living in an ungodly world, and in such circumstances, simple, clear theological truths are inadequate to treat complex problems.

### The Variables in Apocalyptic

Finally, the prophetic genre known as apocalyptic—such as in Daniel, Zechariah, and Revelation—further exemplifies the uncertainty that is inherent to the medium of poetry. In this genre, revelations to the prophets of God's plans in history are couched in the form of visions. These are full of colored horses, warrior angels, composite animals with heads full of horns and horns that have horns, prostitutes giving birth, and dragons that want to eat their children.

Interpretation of apocalyptic literature requires expert familiarity with symbols and their meaning in the ancient thought-world. Even then, there are so many variables that interpreters are forced to speculate.

The book of Revelation is notorious for spawning multiple theories about when the end times are likely to begin, which American president is likely to be the Antichrist, or whether or not feminism is the harlot of Babylon. Major theories about the structure of the book have produced the view that it is sequential and future-oriented (so that we are waiting for a thousand-year reign of Christ on earth before he returns to bring an end to history) or that it is cyclical retellings of the same period of history (so that we are already two-thousand years into the thousand-year reign), and so on.

Given that all of time is present to God, it is surely possible that he could have told his prophets in plain and unambiguous language what would happen and when. The fact that he has chosen to communicate in veiled images and symbols—literature that is supremely indeterminate—is food for thought.

In summary, the presence of poetic literature in the Bible should feature more strongly in our doctrine of Scripture. We fight for the Bible's inerrancy, but inerrancy is a concept that hardly applies to the poetry that makes up as much as 45 percent of the Old Testament's volume. Poetry delights in indeterminacy. It talks in pictures and it places conflicting ideas together without attempting to resolve the difficulties that it creates.

## The Epistles and the Problem of Half-conversations

In Paul's letters and the other epistles, at last we have a genre of literature that is propositional, theological, and that clearly defines logical relationships between its component parts. These books are much more determinate in their use of language—they are discourses that are carefully argued and connected together.

However, even though this literature type is best placed to produce theological certainties, there are still elements that militate against it. Paul makes use of wordplay, often choosing to keep using the same word (such as "flesh" or "law") while shifting what it refers to; for example:

> "I was once *alive apart from the law*, but when the commandment came, sin came alive and I died. The very commandment that promised life proved to be death to me . . . For we know that the law is spiritual, but I am of the flesh, sold under sin . . . So *I find it to be a law* that when I want to do right, evil lies close at hand. For I delight in the law of God, in my inner being, but I see in my members *another law waging war against the law of my mind* and making me captive to the *law of sin* that dwells in my members." (Rom 7:9–10, 14, 21–23)

I can see three or four separable uses of the word "law" in this text and perhaps there are more.

Paul will go on to use "flesh" (which stands for sinful humanness here) in the next chapter in terms of God punishing sin in *Christ's* flesh (8:3). The old NIV translation preferred to translate terminology clearly and consistently, and chose to translate "flesh" as "sinful nature." Consistency in translation in chapter 8:3 meant that they inadvertently implied that Christ had a sinful nature too.

Rom 7 is also an example of a text from the epistles that is notoriously difficult to interpret. Paul seems to adopt a persona in this text, but it is not clear who exactly Paul is speaking as. The "I" in Rom 7 might be Paul as a Christian, as a pre-conversion Jew, as a representative of the human predicament in general, as Adam (Adam could genuinely say "I was once alive apart from the law" [7:9]), and there may be other possibilities. There are many top-level New Testament scholars representing these views, particularly the first two.

The epistles may be speaking clearly, but they are speaking to their *original audience*,[18] not to us,[19] and one of the major problems for us as later interpreters is that no one thought to preserve an account of the problem(s) that prompted the authors to write—something that God could surely have seen to if clarity and certainty were a main concern of his. We only have one side of what was usually a two-sided conversation. The book of Colossians, for example, responds to false teaching from an unknown source. Interpreters differ over whether Col 2:18 ("the worship of angels"), for example, is describing Gentile *worship of angelic beings* or Jewish mysticism by which one was transported into heaven to experience *angelic worship of God*, to mention two major schools of thought. It is hard to know whether we should take it as a warning against idolatry or against Christian mysticism—a very major difference in application!

So, even in the epistles, God has not providentially arranged for his people to have all the necessary information in order to understand the texts that he preserved for us.

In summary, we might *want* a Bible that yields certainty in interpretation, but consideration of what we *actually have* in the Bible suggests that God seems not to prioritize clarity and certainty. Most biblical genres are inherently indeterminate and cultivate the *reader's involvement* in the textual puzzles that they create for us; they are not the sorts of genres one would have chosen if clear, fixed meaning was the aim. If God wanted to, he could have seen to it that sufficient information to produce the correct interpretations was preserved, or that the authorized interpretations of his word were handed down. This seems not to be what he wanted for us.

> "[Our] formulation [of a biblical doctrine] will certainly not give a final or exhaustive account of its subject. *All doctrines terminate in mystery;* for they deal with the works of God, which man in this

---

18. Even to the ancient audiences they still were not necessarily perfectly clear; even Peter calls Paul's letters hard to understand!

19. This is not to say that these letters are not *for* us. We must acknowledge, however, that these are time-bound letters and we are not the intended recipients. Reading ourselves into the pronouns that the writers use can be a distortion in itself.

world cannot fully comprehend, nor has God been pleased fully to explain. 'We know in part'—and only in part."[20]

## The Human Need for Certainty

It seems to me that the indeterminacy of Scripture is well supported by the evidence and yet hard for Christians to accept. For many, the idea of indeterminacy will *feel* wrong. Why would you exchange a view of Scripture that allows you to have certainty for one that calls so many certainties into question?

The short answer is that we should have a view of Scripture that fits the evidence rather than fitting the evidence into a view of Scripture that we prefer—we should shape our views and our certainties on the realities of what we have in the Bible. More than this, certainty might be comfortable, but it might just be destructive of genuine Christianity.

If it is not the nature of the Bible itself that prompts people to insist on its clarity, factuality, and universal applicability, *what is it* that motivates the persistence of this view of Scripture?

### Group Formation and the Closure Spectrum

For some time, psychologists have researched the reasons why people organize into groups—including groups such as churches or seminaries. Apparently, there is a long-standing consensus that the formation of groups is strongly linked to how the group pursues and handles knowledge. There are two major principles that make this link, namely:

- "Individuals' understandings of the world are held as true to the extent that they can be affirmed by some social group."
- "Groups can only exist to the extent that their members have a shared understanding of the world."[21]

These principles mean that individuals seek out and form groups with like-minded people who share and affirm their beliefs. Then, within the group, the uniformity of belief produces a *consensus* that is easily confused with the truth, and which in turn tends to allow subjective matters (opinions

20. Packer, *"Fundamentalism,"* 75–76.
21. Kruglanski and Orehek, *The Need for Certainty*, 3–4.

or attitudes) to be elevated the status of correct thinking or objective knowledge.

Conspiracy theorists provide us with a good example of this. A conspiracy theory arises when someone develops an alternative explanation for the evidence related to a certain phenomenon. Perhaps a secret-service agent seemed to move *before* the president was shot, rather than in *response* to it, and the theorist sets out to provide a reconstruction that places this agent at the center of an assassination plot. Although this begins as a matter of speculation, the story appeals to the members of the theorist's *Dungeons and Dragons* guild, and as more and more people join in with this theory and affirm it as a possibility, it soon takes on the status of a *probability*. Representatives of the official explanation might call it nonsense, but *they would, wouldn't they!* They're only trying to shut down the new theory because they're part of the cover-up.

Kruglanski and Orehek explain that a lot of our group-forming behavior is attributable to a psychological preference for what they call *the need for cognitive closure*. They define the need for closure as "the desire for a quick and firm answer to a question and the aversion toward ambiguity or uncertainty."[22]

The need for closure ranges along a spectrum, with individuals with a strong desire for closure at one end, and those with avoidance of closure at the other. Those who have a low need for closure are likely to court the opinions of others and consider a variety of views, perhaps refusing ever to come to a conclusion; those who have a high need for closure will look to a strong answer from within the group—one that resolves the problem quickly and is *satisfying enough*.

## *Characteristics of High-closure Behavior*

For many people, certainty is experienced as a reward, whereas uncertainty (especially about one's future) is experienced as a threat or virtually as pain.

> "Your brain detects something is wrong, and your ability to focus on other issues diminishes. Your brain doesn't like uncertainty—it's like a type of pain, something to be avoided. Certainty on the other hand feels rewarding, and we tend to steer toward it, even when it might be better for us to remain uncertain."[23]

---

22. Kruglanski and Orehek, *The Need for Certainty*, 4.
23. Rock, *Hunger for Certainty*.

Because people with a high need for closure experience a pleasure-or-pain response to open questions or doubt about the future, they want resolution as quickly as possible—its lack only prolongs the sense that they are under threat.

The need for closure is an *emotional* drive (one that its owner is often unaware of), rather than a drive that is rational. Because of the role that closure plays in group formation, people who have this emotional need gravitate to kinds of groups that are best tooled to service it. They will form bonds where the group:

- shows consensus of opinion;
- prefers leaders who make confident, unambiguous decisions; and
- resists the influence of anyone who disrupts the group's shared reality or tries to reopen matters that were considered settled.

Such groups tend to be conservative in ideology and traditional in their practices because this is a means by which to preserve their identity. They tend to prefer autocratic leaders and stricter boundaries between insider and outsider, because such leaders provide answers and such boundaries insulate the group from divergent opinions or criticism. People who hold opinions against the consensus of the group are treated with suspicion or hostility, because it most easily resolves the emotional threat response that they provoke.[24]

A series of studies was conducted to test whether a greater sense of external threat increased the participants' need for cognitive closure. For example, they showed one group a slide-show related to the 9/11 terror attacks, and another group a benign video about the facilities at Google. Those shown the more threatening video tested significantly higher in a subsequent need-for-closure test than the control group.[25] A greater perceived threat from the outside heightens our need for resolution of that tension, and it amplifies the sense that the in-group is safe and right and in need of protection.

---

24. Kruglanski and Orehek, *The Need for Certainty*, 5–8.
25. Kruglanski and Orehek, *The Need for Certainty*, 10.

## Dangers of High-closure Thinking

Having found that the threat of terror stimulates higher levels of need for closure, Kruglanski and Orehek say:

> "The elevated need for closure enhances group identification, interdependence with others, out-group derogation, and, more specifically, support for tough and decisive counterterrorism policies, and for leaders seen as committed to such policies."[26]

Their research was done in the context of the "war on terror," and so they concluded that perceived threat (of terror attacks) drives approval for a leadership style and for morally questionable behavior that people would ordinarily be far less eager to support—such as the use of torture in interrogation. Christian groups might not be directly interested in counterterrorism, but the church has been a noisy contributor to American politics—engaging in what is often called "culture wars" over issues such as teaching of evolution in schools, prayer in schools, abortion, homosexuality, same-sex marriage, and so on. The idea that Christianity is at war for the soul of the nation and for its own survival is common.

War-time rhetoric is useful for Christian teachers and media personalities because it provides a clear cause around which to rally, it puts a face on the enemy, and it motivates the faithful to give their attention, their time, and their money in a way that genuine Christian causes—such as the Great Commission—usually do not. But war-time rhetoric achieves its ends by using fear, and perceived threat drives up the need for closure.

High need for closure is a strong motivator for groups to secure their own status as being in the right and having the truth, but when this is achieved without a genuine spirit of humble enquiry, it has the potential to cultivate extreme and dangerous views. This is because closure depends on strong pressure to agree with one's group—even if the group's reasoning is inconsistent or if it bends the moral rules in its treatment of outsiders.

For example, I wonder how many Christians would have approved of detention camps for children who had been forcibly separated from their parents if it were done by a *foreign* government? But when it's as important as needing to protect your own family from an alleged invasion of criminal immigrants? Then the problem becomes urgent and the moral boundaries

---

26. Kruglanski and Orehek, *The Need for Certainty*, 12.

change. It becomes a "necessary measure"—and besides, kids *love* summer camp![27]

Many of us will have experienced evangelicals in leadership—representatives of Christ's love, grace, and truth—behaving with *hostility* when the disagreement is theological. The usual Christian calling applies when it concerns things that don't matter, but when it comes to theology, the threat must be neutralized.

Kruglanski and Orehek[28] proceed to list the following dangers for the group that prizes closure too highly. It breeds "conformity, obedience, group polarization, groupthink, and the justification of violence [or hostility] against out-groups . . . The lack of attention paid to alternative perceptions and possible courses of action means that these pressures can give rise to inaccuracies in perception, and decisions with disastrous consequences" even when good solutions and answers (outside the group) are available. In other words, an increased sense of threat can cause us to make inaccurate judgements, fail to see different approaches to the problem, and make poor decisions.

Sticking with "the devil you know" makes sense to so many of us because change is inherently uncertain and induces fear that familiar circumstances do not. Aversion to uncertainty means that many people prefer to continue doing what is familiar—or seek answers in the comfortable past—rather than exploring a new approach that might be better or attempting to create new solutions themselves.[29]

Perhaps even more seriously, high-closure thinking is potentially damaging to our evangelistic witness. When we speak confidently but incorrectly about some point that we've become convinced of, it discredits us in the eyes of the watching world, and it risks tarnishing our presentation of the gospel. Furthermore, harsh leadership, superficial piety, and shallow treatment of deep issues are alienating for outsiders. We should want the only obstacle to the gospel to be the outsider's rejection of the gospel itself. Christianity suffers when there is too little humility, honesty, and authenticity.

---

27. For the description of child detention centers as "summer camps", see Wootson, *Fox News's Laura Ingraham*.
28. Kruglanski and Orehek, *The Need for Certainty*, 12–13.
29. Rock, *Hunger for Certainty*.

## Turn Neither Right Nor Left

*High-closure Thinking vs Truth*

Perhaps you have heard warnings of dire consequences such as: "If we don't fight for seven-day creationism, the church will deny the historical Adam, and from there it's only a matter of time before they deny original sin and Christ himself," or: "If we don't insist on keeping the Sunday Sabbath, Christians will get wrapped up in their entertainment and stop going to church altogether."

There undoubtedly are certain teachings or moral compromises that will lead to awful consequences for the church. The problem with arguments from consequences, however, is that the evil that we foresee in our opponent's future doesn't come about nearly as frequently as our arguments claim they will. In fact, whenever someone insists that an outsider's view will lead to some catastrophic result, it's usually because appealing to fear is easier than addressing their actual argument.

The high need for certainty and closure is a psychological preference, but not something that the Bible encourages us to cultivate. On the contrary, the Bible itself is tooled towards indeterminacy, and the idea of faith is that we *trust God* in an uncertain world over which we have precious little control.

The need for certainty and closure is especially problematic for Christians because it is so opposed to the faith, love, hope, and truth that supposedly characterize us.

Consider how the high need for closure threatens truth:

- It produces a preference for leaders who are decisive and autocratic, whereas the acquisition of truth depends on the application of wisdom and knowledge—two qualities that are produced by study, careful reflection, and self-criticism.

- It produces a preference for easy and early answers, whereas complex problems usually require nuanced solutions. Nuance arises out of hard-earned expertise, for which there are no shortcuts.

- It produces a preference for the status quo (because settled solutions are safe space) and resistance to transformation (because change is perceived as threat).

- It insulates the group from correction—whether from the outsider who upsets certainty with unauthorized ideas (and can be considered hostile and unreliable by default), or from the insider who begins to reopen "closed" issues (and needs therefore to be shut down or shut out). Truth, however, is something that must be submitted to, not ruled out of court.

- It makes a virtue of affirmation (of the group or its leaders) rather than reflection (from which self-criticism or deeper thinking might emerge).

In short, high-closure groups are set up to exhibit high confidence, clear answers, and strong identity—all of which might appear to be strengths—but they are also more likely to be hostile towards perceived threats, more likely to lack care and nuance towards sensitive or complex issues, and more likely to be strongly resistant to self-criticism, listening to the views of others, or embracing necessary change.

Christ's mission is transformative; repentance requires self-examination and commitment to submit to truth; Christ commands us to love our enemies and to answer opponents with gentleness and respect. Christ modeled humility and put it forward as a primary virtue and an example for us to follow. This is all contrary to high-closure values.

Even the apparent strengths of high-closure groups (confidence, clarity, strong identity) are not highly prized in Scripture; in fact, the Pharisees—the chief opponents of Jesus and recipients of his strongest rebukes—*exhibited all of these characteristics*. Certainty is less important that trust, and a strong identity is only valuable to the degree that it reflects Christ's character.

Westboro Baptist—a church devoted to the love of Jesus, and owners of the website "godhatesfags.com"—is an easy target for our ridicule and/or utter dismay, but the sad result of their certainty is that they celebrate their own rightness and faithfulness even as they behave towards sinners in precisely the opposite way that Jesus did.

The fact is that *all of us* might be guilty of patting ourselves on the back for "guarding the good deposit" when all that we've done is guarded ourselves from the people that God sent to correct us. If we make a virtue of decisive certainty and stamp out anything that differs from our perception of "God's ways," we risk never finding out that God's ways are not our ways.

It is important for us to have due confidence in the core of our faith, but certainty is in many ways the antithesis of faith.

## Scripture is Divine and Human

Science fiction has often explored the possibility of human contact with transcendent beings. Often—when the films are not about these aliens trying to kill all humans—the film centers on the attempt to communicate. How do we make ourselves understood to creatures that are so unlike us that they don't even use speech?

Spielberg's *Close Encounters of the Third Kind* is a classic of this sort—humans and aliens are able to communicate by learning a code of lights and musical notes. In 2016's *Arrival*, alien ships descend upon major cities around the world and wait. World leaders, fearing the intentions of these strange creatures, become increasingly restless, and eventually, after misunderstanding a communication from the aliens, begin mobilizing for war. Meanwhile, a linguistics professor must decode the alien language that the mist-shrouded heptapods draw in rings of smoke—before it's too late.

In some of these films, such as in 1997's *Contact*, the huge barrier that exists between us and these transcendent beings is bridged by a sort of accommodation to human limitations—an incarnation of sorts. In *Contact*, Jodie Foster's character communicates with an alien power that appears in the form of her father, with whom she can talk freely and without barriers.

## The Bible as a Communication Attempt

While we differ over what precisely the inspiration of Scripture means in practice, evangelicals tend to agree that Scripture is a meaningful communication attempt between a messenger and receivers—it was written by someone who put an intended meaning in writing with a particular reader or readers in mind. As obvious as this might sound, it raises essential questions, such as "*Who* is the intended reader?" and it does have very important implications for where we do and don't find meaning.

If the books of the Bible are messages between an author and a reader, it is important that we understand what that message was *in its context*. None of the books of the Bible were written *to us*. They were preserved *for our benefit*, but we must acknowledge that we read from very different backgrounds and assumptions to those of the original reader. Reading in context means trying to leave our own context and to read like the original recipients would have.

## What the Bible Seems To Be

While the reader is the one *for whom* the text has meaning, this is not to say that the reader *gives* a text its meaning. A text that means anything means nothing. The meaning of a text is the message that the author gave it.[30] The *significance* of that message may differ from reader to reader and age to age, but it is the interpreter's job to try to recover the text's intended meaning before its significance can be judged.

> "A text is an assertion of a human person, transmitted in writing—a person who can no longer defend himself against misunderstanding. Who can step forward as his advocate if not [the interpreter]?[31] Criticism tries, as well as it is able, to preserve the rights of the text, and in its name to counter misinterpretations. Indeed, there is no other possible way of allowing a text, as the word of another person, the freedom to speak for itself."[32]

Even when the New Testament uses a text from the Old, we need to understand the Old Testament text in its own context; having done that, we can then determine how the New Testament is using it. We can't use the New Testament to determine what an Old Testament text means, because sometimes the New Testament is using the Old in creative ways and not *interpreting* its texts at all. For example, when Matt 2:15 claims that Jesus' return from Egypt is a fulfilment of prophecy, he is quoting a text from Hos 11 that is rebuking Israel for only ever falling into idolatry and rebellion. Hos 11:1 is not *about Jesus* because Jesus isn't the rebellious son spoken of there. Most likely, Matthew sees Jesus as the fulfilment of Hosea 11 because he is the start of a new exodus moment. He will redeem people and they will not stray. One cannot understand Matthew's meaning without first recognizing what Hosea meant originally—and seeing in Jesus a *contrast*.

The idea that the meaning of a biblical text remains what it originally meant (though its significance might vary) has implications for inspiration. It means that God inspired a message to readers in a certain time and place; the Bible was written *for* us but not *to* us.

---

30. See Barton, *Biblical Criticism*, 102–103, and Mantzavinos, *Hermeneutics*, 4. Aims of Text Interpretation.

31. The source reads "historical criticism" here, but out of context it would be misleading to render it as such. The book is advocating well-rounded interpretation that makes use of whatever tools aid in recovering meaning in context. At this point the book is arguing that historical work is *needed* in this process, not that it is the *primary mode* of interpretation.

32. Barton, *Biblical Criticism*, 72.

Those who read the Bible as if it were speaking directly to them are effectively taking a reader-response approach to the Bible—meaning becomes something that *you* bring to the text. You might claim that it is *God* speaking directly to you through his word (and, sure, God can do as he pleases), but this has not prevented people from believing and teaching utterly false things from the Bible because of this approach. This is an unevangelical method that can and does lead to interpretive chaos.

If meaning is tied to original context, what does that mean for God's authorship of Scripture? Was *God* restricted to the immediate context of those that he inspired? What about his supernatural knowledge given in prophecy—especially prophecy about the future? Could the prophets speak better than they knew?

On one hand, of course they could. The genre of oracle purports to be direct, mystical communication from God to people. God could clearly inspire things that find their source in his timeless omniscience. Nevertheless, many prophecies that have deep New Testament significance were spoken into a context, had meaning for that time, and were not directly Messianic. For example:

- Isa 7:14 says: "Therefore the Lord himself will give you a sign. Behold, the virgin shall conceive and bear a son, and shall call his name Immanuel." Matt 1 claims this as a prophecy fulfilled by Christ, but Isa 7:17 makes it clear that the fulfilment is imminent: the child in question will barely be weaned before the King of Assyria takes them into exile, and 8:3–4 describes its fulfilment—"the prophetess" conceives.

- Dan 7:13–14 describes "one like a son of man" approaching the Ancient of Days and being given an everlasting kingdom—a prophecy that Jesus applied to himself in his trials (Matt 24 and 26). However, Daniel asks for an interpretation and he is given one. It identifies the ones who receive this kingdom as "the saints":

    "These four great beasts are four kings who shall arise out of the earth. But *the saints of the Most High* shall receive the kingdom and possess the kingdom forever, forever and ever" . . . As I looked, this horn made war with the saints and prevailed over them, until the Ancient of Days came, and judgment was given for the saints of the Most High, and the time came when *the saints possessed the kingdom*. (Dan 7:17–18, 21–22)

So, the fact that God is the one author behind all of the human authors of Scripture does not seem to alter its rootedness in time and culture. We still are committed to understanding it as a divine message planted within human contexts and dependent on its original meaning if we are to understand its future significance.

## The Bible is Sufficient, Not Complete

Bill Bryson is an American author who is best known for his observational humor based on his travels around the world. Bryson turned his hand to a study of the historical development of scientific knowledge and methods, which he called *A Brief History of Nearly Everything*. The title, in spite of its acknowledgement of its own incompleteness, makes a claim that no book could ever seriously make. Even within the naturalistic worldview that considers scientific knowledge to be the only real knowledge, it is still bordering on arrogant to think that one could capture "nearly everything" there is to know.[33]

I mention this because Christians (some consciously and some not) sometimes think of the Bible as God's word on everything—if there is an issue that you're having, the Bible will have the answer to it, and so there are any number of books that claim to be providing the *biblical* view on a subject (such as dating or dieting or dinosaurs). However, this is not a claim that the Bible makes for itself and nor is it something that we can reasonably infer from the kind of material we find in its pages.

The Bible contains principles for wise and godly living, and it is right for us to try to apply these things to diverse circumstances, but there are many things about which the Bible says far too little for us to speak on them with much confidence. For example, there is no statement about the fate of the unborn—I have heard Christians say that they definitely are *not* going to be in heaven because David was "sinful in the womb" and one can only be saved from sin by the gospel, and I have heard some say that the unborn definitely *will* be in heaven, because God is fair and they have performed no actions for God to condemn.

Similarly, we have no information about which system of government is best. Capitalism is often regarded as Christian (perhaps because conservative parties tend to identify as both). In my area, we receive a pamphlet

---

33. I am not accusing Bryson of arrogance here; I am sure he is not making this claim seriously. It is also an excellent read that I highly recommend.

produced by a far-right organization every election time that claims God is for capitalism and that socialism is theft (those are apparently all the choices). On the other hand, there is a growing feeling among other Christian groups that care for the poor should be part of good governance and that social democracy would be a better expression of Christian values.

And what about issues that didn't exist in biblical eras, such as genetic engineering or climate change? It is clear that the Bible says things of importance to these sorts of issues, but it is equally clear that there are a host of issues that biblical information does not directly address or fully solve.

The Bible was not written with the *purpose* of being a complete religious system. The books (or major parts of them) were written individually and brought into smaller collections (such as the Pentateuch or Twelve Prophets) and, eventually, collected into the canon. The books, therefore, exhibit the aims for which they were originally written—even if that purpose was as narrow as urging a master such as Philemon to take back a runaway slave.

To underline this further, consider that there is little in the canon that resembles systematic theology. Books such as Deuteronomy and Romans come closest to "doing theology," but they also have relatively narrow goals. Deuteronomy is seen as an exploration of Israel's covenant obligations summarized in the Ten Commandments, and Romans briefly outlines Paul's gospel for the benefit of Roman Christians whom he has not met but from whom he is requesting missionary support, and it aims also to address a divide that existed between Jewish and Gentile Christians. It covers important issues of sin, justification, the gift of the Spirit and Christian living, but even this limited range of issues is treated in brief and not systematically.[34] The books of the canon do not set out with the intention of covering all the theological ground that we might wish they did.

The Bible rather prioritizes teaching us Christ, so that it establishes a worldview and grows wisdom in us. This in turn enables God's people to image God's character and to exercise good judgement in God's world.

---

34. For example, he says things such as "Therefore, just as sin came into the world through one man, and death through sin, and so death spread to all men because all sinned—for sin indeed was in the world before the law was given, but sin is not counted where there is no law. Yet death reigned from Adam to Moses, even over those whose sinning was not like the transgression of Adam, who was a type of the one who was to come" (Rom 5:12–14). This passage presents us with a number of issues that cry out for explanation (How did all sin in Adam? What does it mean that sin is not counted where there is no law? What is the implication of sin that is not trespass?), and since he wrote, several thousands of pages have been devoted to trying to provide such explanation.

The Bible is not a complete resource that tells us what to think about every matter that concerns us. The Bible is a *sufficient* resource to train us in knowledge of the gospel and patterns of godly living. Paul says:

> "[The sacred writings] are *able to make you wise for salvation* through faith in Christ Jesus. All Scripture is breathed out by God and *profitable for teaching, for reproof, for correction, and for training in righteousness*, that the man of God may be complete, equipped for every good work." (2 Tim 3:15–17)

The goal of Scripture is to make *us* complete, not to be a complete resource for us. As a result, there are many issues that cannot be resolved merely by throwing Bible passages at them. Solutions require human wisdom and responsibility (along with God's providence and the help of the Spirit) that is *trained* by Scripture, not proof-texted by it. It is not only the verses in the Bible relevant to the subject itself that matter—more important still is the biblical pattern of mind that enables us to discern and judge a matter clearly.

I taught theology students a handful of lectures on argument each year, and their papers for this class required the discussion of a selection of ethical issues. One of my favorite questions asked them to discuss whether Christians at this point in history ought to be vegetarian. Although I asked them to consider a range of relevant data, not just biblical, I still received very amusing attempts to make a case exclusively from biblical texts about food. Papers argued on one hand that Jesus gave people fish and attended sacrifices and therefore ate meat himself, and on the other hand that Isa 7 says "curds and honey shall he eat" and so he was a vegetarian. Papers argued that Daniel was more healthy eating vegetables only (in spite of the impression in the book that this is virtually a miracle). Papers said things like: "Say you're a vegetarian your whole life and then on your thirtieth birthday you get hit by a bus and die. How would your vegetarianism have been of help to you then?" (This last example is not relevant, but it still makes me laugh.)

None of these arguments are in the least bit helpful to the question of whether or not we should *now* be vegetarian, because there are factors now at play—concerning environmental damage, global food security, and so on—that were not even a remote possibility in biblical eras and were not ethical considerations. Texts about Jesus eating meat or Daniel eating vegetables have no purchase on these issues.

We are responsible for weighing such matters from the perspective of a biblical *pattern of thought*, not only from direct statements of Scripture, and even still, a single, clear "biblical" approach may not be forthcoming. The Bible is sufficient to achieve its purposes, but simply doesn't provide the "brief answer to nearly everything."

## Transcendence of God and Accommodation to Humanity

Emily Thomas of Durham University's philosophy department asks the question: "Does the size of the universe prove God doesn't exist?" Scientists estimate that there are more than two-trillion *galaxies* in the universe,[35] and our galaxy alone contains approximately a hundred-million stars. The best scientific estimate of the age of the universe is that it is about thirteen-billion years old. Given how insignificant our planet is and how recently humankind came to be, how is it possible that we could matter to a god? Thomas writes:

> "Clearly, there is a discrepancy between the kind of universe we would expect a human-oriented God to create, and the universe we live in. How can we explain it? Surely the simplest explanation is that God doesn't exist."[36]

The size of the universe is incomprehensible to us and from our perspective it *is* absurd to think that God could be interested in such insignificant creatures. However, it is not for us to tell God what he is allowed to find valuable—we find gemstones valuable though they are tiny even in comparison to us. They might be small, but they are rare and beautiful and timeless.

On the other hand, if scientists were to change their *own* human-oriented perspective, this is exactly the kind of universe we might expect God to create. The Bible regularly emphasizes God's transcendence. It implies that he is not limited in power or knowledge or any other capacity—he counts the hairs of our head and keeps track when we lose one. It implies that he is not limited by time or distance or needing to be in one place at a time. In heaven itself, Isaiah has a vision of the angels that attend God, and even though they are without sin or corruption, they must attend him with

---

35. This is a mental picture that might help us to visualize a trillion. Imagine you won a prize that allowed you to spend a million dollars *a day*. How long would you have to live in order to spend a trillion dollars? More than 2,700 years.

36. Thomas, *Size of the Universe*.

faces and feet covered. They are not holy enough to be near him simply by virtue of their createdness and his transcendence as Creator (Isa 6). It was not *harder* for God to create a very big universe than it would have been for him to create a little one with a big Earth in the middle of it. God creates impossibly big things because why not? And he has no obligation to assign value in size-order.

What the size of the universe should tell us is that if there is a God, he is very, very, *very* unlike us. Yes, we are made in his likeness so that we are able to understand relationship with him, but God is so much bigger and so much more powerful than we can begin to comprehend—he outnumbers the million trillions of stars and planets; he cannot be contained even by the far borders of space.

> "Then the LORD answered Job out of the whirlwind and said: 'Who is this that darkens counsel by words without knowledge? . . . Where were you when I laid the foundation of the earth? Tell me, if you have understanding. Who determined its measurements—surely you know! Or who stretched the line upon it? . . . Can you bind the chains of the Pleiades or loose the cords of Orion? Can you lead forth the Mazzaroth in their season, or can you guide the Bear with its children? Do you know the ordinances of the heavens? Can you establish their rule on the earth?'" (Job 38:1–2, 4–5, 31–33)

If this is the God that we have, for him to relate to us requires him to make himself very small.

> "Have this mind among yourselves, which is yours in Christ Jesus, who, though he was in the form of God, did not count equality with God a thing to be grasped, but emptied himself, by taking the form of a servant, being born in the likeness of men. And being found in human form, he humbled himself by becoming obedient to the point of death, even death on a cross." (Phil 2:5–8)

The incomprehensible vastness of the universe reveals the all-surpassing greatness of our God who cannot be controlled and will not be tamed. The humility of our God who by us and for us was humiliated reveals a God who in his inner being is other-centered love, and who thus willingly condescends to know us, even though it makes no sense.

> "What is man that you are mindful of him,
> and the son of man that you care for him?" (Ps 8:4)

To those who have no claim to know God or to rest in his presence, he nevertheless says:

> "I said, 'You are gods,
> sons of the Most High, all of you.'" (Ps 82:6)

Or as the fourth-century church father Athanasius provocatively put it:

> "God became man that man might become God."[37]

The incarnation is such an astonishing miracle (for ancient people no less than for us) because the uncontainable God allowed himself to be contained by time, space, and human limitations. How this could be and what really went on in the meeting of human weakness and divine power remains something of a mystery—one that theologians have wrestled with since it happened. Nevertheless, Christ as the supreme Word of God submitted himself to flesh and became man.

Scripture as the word of God that bears witness to Christ is similarly a meeting of divine power and human limitation, and the "incarnation" of the written word of God similarly remains a mystery. Whatever one says about the nature of Scripture, it gives us a vision of this transcendent God, but not full access to God as he is. Scripture is an *accommodation* to humanity and to the form of human thought—it is God's word made small enough for us.[38] God makes himself smaller in order to communicate with us.

The sorts of images that God uses for himself are illustrative of how God has accommodated knowledge of himself to our humanity. He is Father, but not in the way that means there is a divine mother. He is spoken of in the masculine, but not so that it is inappropriate to use feminine metaphors of himself too.[39] God is described as having hands and other anthropomorphic features, but he is also spirit, invisible, and "dwells in unapproachable light" (1 Tim 6:16).

---

37. Athanasius, *De Incarnatione Verbi Dei*, 38 [54.3]. https://www.monergism.com/incarnation-ebook.

38. "If God's eternality means that his historical presence exceeds any temporal event, and indeed that the human relationship to God always strains human language, then the reporting of an event by a biblical author seems to involve more than mere historical accuracy. And there is possibly a sense in which factual accuracy may need to be subordinated to a more poetic rendering of an event so that its significance is grasped." (Merrick and Garrett, "Introduction," 20)

39. For example, Deut 32:18; Isa 42:14, 49:15, 66:13; Hos 13:8 (the bear robbed of cubs is usually taken to be female); and Matt 23:37.

Scripture is similarly accommodated to humanity. God could presumably have shown us himself in a mystical or gnostic way—bypassing the frailties of words and arguments, and inserting a divine vision of himself directly into the spirits of his people. However, he has chosen rather to shrink and constrain his self-revelation so that his word became fitted for human minds, time-bound cultures, ordinary human language, and ordinary human conventions and genres. It might be more than that, but it is *at least* that.

John Woodridge, critiquing a proposal that the Bible should be seen as admitting errors in peripheral matters, said:

> "God accommodated Himself to our human weakness and limited capacity to understand His thoughts by communicating to us through human words . . . [The] authors of Scripture . . . did not reflect upon truth with the same categories of Western logic that are familiar to us. They were not concerned to describe historical and 'scientific' items with great accuracy. In consequence, what we moderns consider to be the small 'errors' committed by the Bible's human authors do not detract from biblical authority, for the Bible's authority is not associated with its form of words but with Christ and His salvation message to which the words point."[40]

God transcends the limits of time and space, but his chosen means of revealing himself does not. He provides us what is needed, in our humanness, to know enough of him and his plan of salvation that we can find ourselves in relationship with him—albeit one that is as if perceived in a mirror dimly.

The incarnation of Christ is a useful analogy for the divine-human nature of Scripture too,[41] because just as imbalances in how Christ was both God and man led to heresies—for example, Apollinarianism and Docetism, which over-emphasized his divinity at the expense of his humanity, or Ebionism and Adoptionism, which over-emphasized his humanity over his divinity—so also Scripture should not be seen as divine at the expense of its humanity (e.g., the dictation model) or merely a human book about

---

40. Woodbridge, *Biblical Authority*, 21.

41. Although this shouldn't be pushed too far. Scripture is not a person and it is not an object of worship as Christ is. If it emerged that some or other element in Scripture were proven to be error, it would not force us to believe that Christ therefore might also have been sinful (as if defect in one implied defect in the other). The way in which humanity met divinity in Scripture need not be fully comparable to the meeting of God and man in Christ.

the search for God at the expense of its divinity (e.g., liberal and naturalistic models).

Although the Bible is breathed out by our transcendent God, its human nature means that it has been subjected to the boundaries of time and space, and many of the limitations of human speech and thought. Its inspiration means that it is the document that God intends it to be and that it will achieve the revelatory purposes for which he intended it. However, just as Christ in the incarnation laid aside his majesty, the inspiration of Scripture most likely does *not* mean that we may ascribe to it attributes that properly belong to the eternal and transcendent God.

## Divine-human Scripture and Fallible Interpretation

In my circles, it is common for service leaders to introduce the preacher by saying something like: "Now we're going to hear from the Lord," or: "Now we are going to hear God speak." In one sense, of course, this is true. Scripture is the word of God and we believe that God does speak to people through it. However, it suggests that God's words and the preacher's words are more closely related than they really are.[42]

When the New Testament warns about false teachers, very often it is implied that these are people from *within the church*, not outside it. We are, after all, far more suspicious of the outsider and primed to expect false teaching "out there"; it's far harder to recognize when the false teacher is just known to you as *the teacher!* But experience itself provides evidence on a weekly basis that even normally orthodox preachers are not supernaturally empowered in the pulpit and prevented from speaking incorrect or misleading things.

One of my favorite viral-video buffoons is a preacher from a church called "Faithful Word." He was evidently inspired by the biblical description of men as those "that pisseth against the wall" (e.g., 1 Kgs 21:21, KJV). While visiting Germany, he had become incensed at signs in restrooms that prohibited men from urinating standing up. Seeing as one can't urinate against a wall while sitting down, he was angry that the Germans were depriving him of his God-given responsibility as a man to splash the toilet

---

42. I recognize that 1 Pet 4:11 encouragers speakers to speak as those who speak the utterances of God and servers to serve as if by God-given strength. The focus, however, is on using gifts for God's glory (i.e., to recognize God's labor behind our own efforts), not on the authority with which one engages in their exercise.

seat from a height. Here is a short section of what is an enormously enjoyable sermon:

> "But I was reading the Bible and I kept seeing this phrase, and I studied this phrase in the Bible, and it's used six times, and it's used by God. It's used out of the mouth of God . . . Him that pisseth against the wall? You see that in the Bible. It's used six times in the Bible . . . And you'll say, 'Aw, I can't believe you speak that way, it's vile'. Well, I'm sorry, but the Bible says that the words of Jesus Christ are wholesome words, and the Bible says every word of God is pure, so don't accuse me of using bad language. That's what the Bible says. He said, 'I will destroy him that pisseth against the wall.' . . . And by the way, that expression is only used in the King James Bible. The New King James eliminates it. This is what the New King James says. [Adopts effeminate nasal tone] *'Males'*. 'All the *males*'. And, you know, the guys who made it, they are *males*. They're not men. And God said, a man *is somebody who pisses against the wall* . . . OK. I was in Germany, and I went to use the restroom in Germany, in several different peoples' houses, I mean, totally different people. And even in public places they had a sign that prohibited a man from peeing standing up! . . . I was like, 'Is that a joke? It's kind of a crude joke.' [My wife] said, 'It's not a joke.' She said, 'No man in Germany pees standing up.' . . . That's where we're headed in this country, my friend! We've got a bunch of pastors who pee sitting down!"[43]

Whole books could be written about the wrong turns on display in this sermon, but even the name of the church declares an expectation of a *faithful word*. I assume that the pastor is a Spirit-filled brother and someone eager to serve God whole-heartedly, but all the same, his sermon that Sunday was about as far from the word of God as a well-meaning preacher can get.

Why are our words in preaching not identifiable with the word of God? It is because the acts of translating, reading, and teaching the Bible are all modes of *interpretation*. Our preaching is interpretive, not the unmediated word of God. While God might speak to people through us, our preaching is unfortunately (but most certainly) the word of man. Interpretation of the Bible unavoidably means that we read the Bible from our own assumptions, prejudices, and preferences. Exegetical techniques exist to mitigate much of the subjectivity—and this is why responsible theological training is essential—but some always remains.

---

43. Pickering, *Pee Pastor*.

One of my favorite quotes of all time is this one from Upton Sinclair:

> "It is difficult to get a man to understand something when his salary depends on his not understanding it."

Sinclair perfectly captures the human tendency to let our needs and wants interfere with the truth. Our motivations in life and in biblical interpretation are never as pure as we like to make out. When truths are inconvenient, we are more likely to continue preferring the mistake.[44]

The Bible is the authoritative word of God, but interpretation is a *human discipline* that admits as much variation and error as any other. The Chicago Statements affirm that extrabiblical disciplines are able to correct human interpretation of Scripture for this reason. It is *essential* that Bible interpreters recognize the fallibility of their task. One is on shaky ground when one insists that some area of knowledge or a secular finding is wrong because it disagrees with the Bible, because even though we believe that the Bible is completely true, all disagreements are between *interpretations* of God's word and God's world. God's world and his word both speak God's truth; science and biblical study both are human processes of interpretation attempting to get at that truth.

> "We are increasingly becoming aware that the authority of Scripture is, and must be, mediated to us through the interpretation of Scripture, and that the latter is a human and inexact science."[45]

Subjectivity in the way that we read Scripture is one thing, but there is even more indeterminacy awaiting us in our attempts to *apply* Scripture.

R. T. France wrote *Women in the Church's Ministry* to demonstrate that interpreters with a high view of Scripture and applying good principles of exegesis faithfully to the text nevertheless arrive at conflicting theological positions. Part of the problem, he says, is that evangelicals have often assumed that once one has properly exegeted a text, the modern application of it will be *self-evident*.[46] This is not the case. There are texts—France

---

44. There is a related fallacy of argument known as the fallacy of sunk costs. It points out that even after investors (of whatever kind) have realized that their plan will never achieve the goal that they were pursuing, they will often continue investing in it because they have already spent so much. What do you do as a Christian teacher when you've built your ministry on a particular issue and you then discover that you're most probably wrong?

45. France, *Women*, 15

46. France, *Women*, 12.

suggests Paul's instruction to submit to governing authorities—about which there is little or no exegetical dispute, and yet a variety of opinions on how one is to practice them in modern life.

The denomination to which I belong prides itself in maintaining a high view of Scripture and a high degree of interpretive rigor, and yet for decades we have also acknowledged, as an aside, that we are "weak at application" of Scripture. Under *Apartheid*, this same denomination saw its responsibility to preach the gospel and to *stay out* of politics. The naïveté of this decision was exposed—much as with evangelical advocates of slavery in the American South a century before—in our teaching about the doctrine of *Apartheid*. The Reformed Afrikaans church had declared *Apartheid* to be the will of God, and our branch of the Anglican Church did not disagree. Rather, using biblical texts and the Bible's lack of condemnation for slavery, it claimed that the system of *Apartheid* was within God's will, and the problem with it was the *way in which it was practiced*. If white leaders were godly and generous, there would be no fault.

In 1982, The World Alliance of Reformed Churches declared that *Apartheid* is a heresy.[47] It took as long as a decade after the end of *Apartheid* for a synod of this evangelical church to recognize its role in the past system and to issue an apology for it. You will now struggle to find any evangelical who continues to argue that *Apartheid* could have been compatible with Christian theology.

Because our exegesis of texts is influenced by our own subjectivity, and even more so because our modern *application* of texts involves empathy and intuition (rather than a purely objective method), even interpreters with the highest of evangelical convictions produce much theological variation. There are clear commands in Scripture that most of us nevertheless knowingly ignore (at least in the form in which they were given). Jesus gives an example that he tells us to follow: we must wash one another's feet (John 13:14–15). Paul commands women to cover their heads in worship and commands men not to (1 Cor 11:4–6)—an instruction that we sometimes completely invert by putting hats on bishops. Paul ends four of his letters with the command to greet one another with a holy kiss—something that my aunt attempts to practice but which I vehemently oppose (and most churches seem to take my side).

---

47. Giles, *Justifying Injustice*.

Scripture was written to an audience into whose culture and patterns of thought God's word was imbedded. Scripture has been preserved *for* us who live in new cultural contexts and with different patterns of thought than the original authors. This does not plunge us into interpretive chaos, but it does force us to recognize that many of our interpretive certainties are artificial and that deep humility before our Creator is a far more appropriate response.

## Conclusion

What conclusions should we draw from this?

The Scriptures that we *want* would most likely give us a set of unambiguous beliefs and practices, and the words would be clearly and easily comprehensible to us without having to study and struggle and wonder and disagree. Where disagreement manifests, we could easily point out who the compromiser is.

The Scriptures that we *have*, on the other hand, employ various creative genres that resist neat categorization and full clarity. They seem rather to enjoy ambiguity and provocation. The Bible is true, but it does not for that reason consist of clear, factual material. On the contrary, we have Scriptures that were inspired within specific cultural and literary patterns, some of which are lost to history or at least foreign to modern readers. The biblical text is the word of God, but its authors are human. The Bible is God's revelation of himself, but it is shrunk down to accommodate the divine mind to finite human minds and cultures.

Therefore, how we understand the divine nature of Scripture should not be presumptuous. The Bible is exactly the book that God wanted us to have, but God's inspiration does not usually seem to have over-written human faculties or knowledge. If the Bible is inspired by God, then it was God's intention to give us indeterminacy—these are the kinds of Scriptures that he wanted written and preserved for us. We shouldn't be forcing Scripture into a model that assumes that clear, perfect propositional revelation is what God ought to have given us. God could have communicated unambiguously, but he chose poetry and narrative and apocalyptic instead. If this is so, then difficulties and ambiguities and inconsistencies are perhaps not always there to be resolved, but also inhabited, puzzled over, discussed.

It is true that much of the interpretive diversity that we see in the Christian world has arisen because many churches are suspicious of study, or because they apply interpretive techniques that do nothing to limit the subjectivity of the reader and produce shallow or idiosyncratic teachings. We could arrive at much greater theological unity if we were unified in our commitment to use good exegetical methods. Nevertheless, the indeterminate nature of our incarnate Scriptures will always leave us with questions that cannot be decisively answered by exegesis. The study of God always terminates in mystery.

Theology, therefore, is something that must be held as provisional, not certain. There are some tenets of our faith that are so well-established and so important as to be virtually certain, but many others are so unclear as to be visible only as shapes in the fog. The study of Scripture, new knowledge and fresh thinking, discussion, and diversity all serve to deepen and refresh our understanding of God and his word.

The *Scriptures that we have* ought to provoke in us an appreciation of the deep and multifaceted nature of truth; they should prompt in us a life-long posture of teachability (because there is always more to learn); they should humble us before our own incapacity and need for God's wisdom; and—perhaps most importantly—they should inspire in us love for those who disagree with us. We might own Bibles, but as confident as we might be in our own traditions and interpretations, none of us possesses full insight into the mind of God. Love those who disagree with you, because God disciplines those he loves, and no one ever learns of their errors of judgement from those who unconditionally agree with them.

CHAPTER 5

# The Gospel Center

*He is the beginning, the firstborn from the dead, that in everything he might be preeminent. For in him all the fullness of God was pleased to dwell, and through him to reconcile to himself all things, whether on earth or in heaven, making peace by the blood of his cross. (Col 1:18b–20)*

IF SCRIPTURE IS NOT the matter-of-fact source of crystal-clear theological formulations that we might have hoped it would be, and if by contrast it is a document that is imbedded in human time and culture, and intentionally offers ambiguity and interpretive struggle, how *do* we avoid chaos? On what is our faith based?

At risk of repeating ground we have already covered, evangelicals rightly uphold Scripture as the source of theology and the ultimate authority for Christian belief and practice. However, often without realizing it, evangelicals wrongly move Scripture into the center of our theology.

Our thinking runs as follows. All of our knowledge of God and salvation comes from the Bible—many institutions begin teaching systematic theology with the doctrine of Scripture for this reason. If everything comes from there, then naturally it ought to be the *foundation stone* on which all theology is built.[1] However, a foundation stone needs to be secure, or else the edifice that it supports is liable to collapse. Therefore, the Bible must be divinely inerrant and accurate in every detail, or else it calls into question

---

1. This might be an unacknowledged premise, but the mere act of putting the doctrine of Scripture first can be enough to imply that it is also doctrinally *primary*.

our doctrine of God, and everything else that we've built upon it. If Scripture is anything less than clear and reliable, our faith might fall.

The problem with this kind of thinking about the place of Scripture is that it muddles two things together that should be kept separate: the Bible is the *source* of our knowledge of God, but the foundation stone that *it points us to* is something or someone else.

Think of it like a map. Generally speaking, no one possesses a map to have a map—it exists to guide us to a certain destination. It points beyond itself to the more important thing. It would miss the point to insist that a map must be a perfect reflection of every contour of the path to that destination; the map must get you there. But getting there is the important thing.

In the same way, the Bible points to a certain "destination" and it must be *true* in order for it to be that spiritual "map," but the Bible doesn't have to bear more weight than that.

Rather than placing inerrancy—or even the doctrine of Scripture—at the head of our theological systems, we should acknowledge the central thing that the study of Scripture illuminates for us: Jesus Christ and his gospel.

Some might object that the Bible *is* the gospel (or at least contains it), but to put it another way, if the goal of the Bible is knowledge of God, then it is not sufficient to *know the Bible*. It is pointing us to something beyond itself—to a relationship with God and a way of life to match. In the same way, the center of evangelical theology is not faith in the Bible, but *biblical faith*—faith in the God revealed in the Bible.

## What is the Gospel?

If there is one thing that you would expect evangelical Christians to be able to articulate clearly and easily, it is the answer to the question: "What is the gospel?" After all, we believe that the gospel is the most important message in all of history; it is transformative (often radically) of the life of the one who accepts it; it is the key to life's meaning; it is what defines us as people.

At the theological college at which I trained, this was a question that was posed as an assignment to final-year students, and the goal was to state simply (and to defend) what the gospel message is and what it isn't. In spite of it being basic to everything that we are, every year it provoked fresh discussion and disagreement. It is not hard to identify what we as Christians are about and to list all sorts of issues of importance to us; what *is* hard is to decide what of our beliefs belong to the central message, and what should be left aside as secondary.

According to the definition in the *Evangelical Dictionary of Theology*, to be an evangelical means that we affirm the *central beliefs* of historical Christianity.[2] As a summary of the beliefs that are central to Christianity, Pierard and Elwell cite 1 Cor 15:1–4; specifically they say:

> "Christ died for our sins, was buried, and rose again on the third day in fulfilment of the prophetic Scriptures and thereby provided a way of redemption for sinful humanity."[3]

This description of the gospel has the advantage of being like Paul's own summary, but it should be borne in mind that this is not Paul's *only* summary of the gospel, and standing on its own, it is not reflective of all that Scripture has to say about the matter.[4] Of course Christ's death and resurrection is rightly part of any definition, but one doesn't have to look hard to find crucial gospel doctrines that are missing from this statement. As it is, for example, the statement could happily be used to show that *all people* are saved by Christ's death. There is no mention in this text that we receive salvation by God's grace, or that there is a need for repentance and faith, or that it results in adoption into God's family through the gift of the Holy Spirit—all core components of Paul's message elsewhere. There is also no mention of the Lordship of Christ that makes a demand on our way of life.

If we were to try to find a concise summary of the gospel that Jesus proclaimed, Mark 1:15 is a good candidate:

> "The time is fulfilled, and the kingdom of God is at hand; repent and believe in the gospel."

Jesus claims that the gospel is tied up with repentance and faith in the fulfilment of God's kingdom—a gospel that does not explicitly mention his coming death and resurrection on which Paul focuses and with which Mark's Gospel ends.

Jesus' message about the kingdom being *fulfilled* requires that there is an unfulfilled gospel that has been worked out in Israel's past and which he has come to bring to completion. Any summary of the gospel, therefore,

---

2. Pierard and Elwell, "Evangelicalism," 407.
3. Pierard and Elwell, "Evangelicalism," 407.
4. Admittedly, the authors do not claim that this statement is exhaustive of everything that is central to the gospel, but nor do they do much to supplement it.

needs to take all these factors into account—it is a plan rooted in the Old Testament story; it concerns the establishment of God's kingdom; and its fulfilment comes via the life, death, and resurrection of Jesus Christ.

I would suggest that a canonical summary of the gospel might look something like this:

1. Humans were created to be in relationship with God; the ideal of "God with us" (*immanuel*) runs throughout Scripture.

2. Human rebellion against God's terms of relationship with him led to the expulsion of humanity from his presence (in Eden), and the intrusion of sin and death into human life.

3. The Old Testament promises and covenants described new terms of relationship for his redeemed people in the land that he prepared for them (a new Eden), and his temple represented *immanuel* once again. However, human hearts continued to stray because of the persistence of sin, the temple was destroyed, and Israel was exiled from their land (a new loss of Eden).

4. The New Covenant was inaugurated by a once-for-all sacrifice of God's own son (the ultimate *Immanuel*) in order to deal with sin in human hearts, and Christ's resurrection signals victory over death.

5. The gift of the Holy Spirit seals the New Covenant (the new relational terms) in the hearts of those who are called and who repent and believe, and the Spirit enables us to live eternal life in the present and beyond death.

6. The goal of the gospel is God-with-us in the New Creation (the ultimate Eden).

Because the gospel message involves so many parts, it is difficult to provide a summary that captures everything in one short statement. This is why Paul's gospel in 1 Cor 15 is a *true* summary but not a *complete* summary, and this is why his summaries differ elsewhere, depending on the circumstances into which he was writing.

For these reasons, we should be careful not to say that the Christian gospel *is* the death and resurrection of Jesus. Of course this is good news—and the way in which good news is possible for humankind—but if we limit our gospel to the death and resurrection, it is only good news *for Jesus*. The gospel is good news for *us* too, and so we must add that, by the Spirit, Jesus' death is the means by which we can be redeemed from sin and death too.

But if we leave it there, it makes the good news about *our survival*, which it isn't. We must add that the good news is our eventual deliverance into the presence of God—heaven is not about "going to a better place"; it is about inheriting God himself.[5] But if we leave it there, it makes the good news only about the *life to come*, which it isn't. We must add that we were delivered from sin and corruption; new life in Christ—and his vision of the kingdom—is something that we possess in part *even now*, and which means living out and spreading the good news.[6]

The gospel is perhaps most succinctly captured in the word *immanuel*, God with us. God himself stepped into time and space, and secured for humankind an inheritance in the presence of God that cannot be undone, and (uniquely in all religion) rooted our faith in history. It highlights the centrality of Christ as God incarnate—God's chosen cornerstone on whom the gospel is founded—and it highlights the resulting temple into which we are "being built together into a dwelling place for God by the Spirit" (Eph 2:22). This is the goal that makes the gospel good news for us—unending fullness of life in God's presence.[7]

Recovering our gospel center means a recovery of our commitment to know God in Christ, to live in and for his presence, and to imitate God as agents of reconciliation in the world.

## Christ as the Living Word of God

Coming from a Pentecostal-ish church growing up and moving into an evangelical Anglican church in my twenties, I struggled to fit in with the

---

5. "When Jesus had spoken these words, he lifted up his eyes to heaven, and said, 'Father, the hour has come; glorify your Son that the Son may glorify you, since you have given him authority over all flesh, to give eternal life to all whom you have given him. And this is eternal life, that they know you the only true God, and Jesus Christ whom you have sent.'" (John 17:1–3)

6. "But in another sense, eternal (and thus immortal) life begins as people eat the bread of life (believe in Jesus; John 6:48–51) and so participate in the divine nature (2 Pet. 1:4)" (Johnson, "Life," 643–4). Eph 2:1–10 also pairs death and walking in sin, and life in Christ and walking in good works; this suggests that eternal life begins with transformed living in this world.

7. See also the gospel summary based on Christ as cornerstone in 1 Pet 2:1–12. It too emphasizes that Christ is the cornerstone and we are being built into a spiritual house and a royal priesthood so that we can dwell with God as his people. Note too that this contains responsibilities to offer spiritual sacrifices (2:5), to proclaim God's excellencies (2:9), and to be witnesses to our persecutors by our honorable conduct (2:12).

relative formality of prayer books and other liturgical traditions. One thing that initially struck me as weird was the formula you're supposed to say after the Bible has been read. When the Bible reader is done, they say: "This is the word of the Lord," to which the congregation is meant to reply: "Thanks be to God." Automatic behavior seemed irrational to me, almost as if certain phrases were faith-based Manchurian Candidate triggers, and everybody stopped being people for a minute. Nowadays I usually mumble the formula happily along with the 40 percent of the congregation that is on board with such things. In fact, I even get righteously indignant when the reader messes it up and says: "This is the word of God," because that's not how it goes and now that you've said "God" at the end, I can't very well also say "God"—it sounds clumsy—but the rest of the congregation isn't primed to switch our response to "Thanks be to the Lord." And so those of us who know how things ought to be are left wincing as now only 20 percent of the congregation responds and by artlessly rhyming "God" with "God."

I bring this up not only because liturgical-formula users should be spurred on to greater vigilance, but also because it demonstrates the degree to which we are wired to associate "the word of God" first and foremost with Scripture. Of course Scripture *is* the word of God, but the New Testament itself doesn't usually use "the word" in this way. Far more often, it refers to the effective word of Christ and to the message of the gospel.

- For example, in John 15:3, Jesus declares his disciples clean "because of the word that I have spoken to you."

- In Acts 4:1-4, Peter and John are arrested because they were "proclaiming in Jesus the resurrection from the dead," and many "heard the word" and believed. In Acts 4:31, after they are released, the disciples all commit to "speak the word of God with boldness." This suggests that the word is the message of Jesus and the resurrection (his and ours).

- Acts 6:7 and 12:24 speak about the word of God *increasing*, which would seem to mean that the gospel was gaining new disciples. In Acts 8:14 and 11:1, it talks about the Samaritans and the Gentiles *receiving* the word of God, which would seem to mean that they had received Christ and believed the gospel (see also 1 Cor 14:36).

- In 1 Thess 2, Paul speaks about his gospel preaching among them, calling it "the gospel of God" (e.g., 2:9) and "the word of God" (2:13).

- In 2 Tim 2:8–9, Paul's message is: "Remember Jesus Christ, risen from the dead, the offspring of David, as preached in my gospel, for which I am suffering, bound with chains as a criminal. But the word of God is not bound!" Here "the word of God" is synonymous with "my gospel." In Titus 2:4, he similarly encourages godly behavior, so that "the word of God may not be reviled."

What this illustrates is that when the New Testament speaks about the word of God, we might have in mind the Bible, but the writers are often speaking more particularly about the message of the gospel. They have in mind the *core of the faith*, which they variously identify as the word of grace, the word of faith, the word of life, the word of the kingdom, and the word of the cross. It's the salvation message of Christ as redeemer, Immanuel, and Lord that we are urged to guard and keep and pass on.

This is not to say that the peripheral things in Scripture are *unimportant*, but the New Testament does seem to distinguish between the gospel center that should be kept and guarded, and those things that are matters of dispute or the words, myths, and "endless genealogies" over which Christians might quarrel (see 1 Tim 1:4 and Titus 3:9). The Bible itself tells us the purpose of its writings: it is explicitly so that we would know the Christ, the eternal, Living Word of God:

> "Then he said to them, 'These are my words that I spoke to you while I was still with you, that everything written about me in the Law of Moses and the Prophets and the Psalms must be fulfilled.' Then he opened their minds to understand the Scriptures, and said to them, 'Thus it is written, that the Christ should suffer and on the third day rise from the dead, and that repentance and forgiveness of sins should be proclaimed in his name to all nations, beginning from Jerusalem.'" (Luke 24:44–47)

> "These are written so that you may believe that Jesus is the Christ, the Son of God, and that by believing you may have life in his name." (John 20:31)

> "From childhood you have been acquainted with the sacred writings, which are able to make you wise for salvation through faith in Christ Jesus." (2 Tim 3:15)

Reading the Bible evangelically, therefore, is not primarily about inerrancy or any other theory of the divine-human nature of Scripture. The Bible points us to its cornerstone, its center. Our reading and interpretation of the Bible has the goal of teaching us *Christ and his gospel*. The center of Bible interpretation should be the revelation of and relationship with the Living Word.

Evangelicalism urgently needs to recover its Center. The gospel message is not just about clearing our slate and avoiding judgement. It is not just about securing paradise when we die and avoiding hell. It is not at all about displays of personal piety. It is a message that frees us, that reconnects us with our Creator, and that transforms us and the world around us from the inside. Or at least it should.

It is deeply ironic that the manner in which we defend the fringe matters of the *written* word is often ugly enough to be a distortion of the image of the Living Word to whom it points us. If we *truly* centered our evangelical faith on the gospel message, rather than our "evangelical distinctives," or our fear of the heathens encroaching on our peace and security, or our political allegiances, we would care more about integrity, more about love for our enemies, and more about being agents of transformation in our world. In short, we would actually *be distinctive*, rather than just telling people that we are.

## Chapter 6

# Reading Christ

*"And the Father who sent me has himself borne witness about me. His voice you have never heard, his form you have never seen, and you do not have his word abiding in you, for you do not believe the one whom he has sent. You search the Scriptures because you think that in them you have eternal life; and it is they that bear witness about me, yet you refuse to come to me that you may have life." (John 5:37–40)*

EMANUEL SWEDENBORG WAS A Swedish Lutheran writer who styled himself as a prophet and revelator. His writings are regarded by some sects as having the same authority as the Bible. While some of his contemporaries apparently struggled to see any relevance in the Old Testament, Swedenborg claimed to have the key to unlocking its spiritual riches. Of the seven days of creation, he said:

> "From the mere letter of the Word of the Old Testament no one would ever discern the fact that this part of the Word contains deep secrets of heaven . . . The Christian world, however, is as yet profoundly unaware of the fact that all things in the Word . . . down to the most minute iota, signify and enfold within them spiritual and heavenly things, and therefore the Old Testament is but little cared for."[1]

---

1. Swedenborg, *Arcana Coelestia*, Chapter 1.

## Reading Christ

His interpretation of the seven days of Gen 1 is that they are less about the nature of God and his world and more about "successive states of the regeneration of man." In summary, he interprets them like this:

Day 1. The darkness represents the spiritual darkness in which all exist before regeneration. The spirit of God begins moving upon the face of their waters.

Day 2. Separation of sea and land represents a distinction being made between those things which are of the Lord (such as faith), and those which belong to man (such as the things of the flesh and the world), and which must die before faith can be entered.

Day 3. The sprouting of plants on dry ground represents repentance, which starts to produce good works.

Day 4. The "two luminaries" represent a person's growth in love and illumination by faith.

Day 5–6. The next days represent growth, which by degree produces living creatures. Finally, there is a conflict between the spiritual life that is growing within, and the natural, physical life without, and when love gains the dominion and spiritual things win, a person becomes a "celestial man" (presumably referring to "the image of God").

Day 7. He says: "Those who are being regenerated do not all arrive at this state. The greatest part, at this day, attain only the first state; some only the second; others the third, fourth, or fifth; few the sixth; and scarcely anyone the seventh."

It's quite ingenious, and quite hard to argue against, except to say that there is no reason for thinking any of this. There is nothing in the text that suggests it is an illustration of the spiritually actualized person. Allegorical interpretations of Scripture such as that of Swedenborg have led to much misunderstanding; there *are* biblical allegories (such as the Parable of the Sower), but when we force them onto the text, we are in fact denying that there is inspiration of the *ideas* of the authors. God inspired them to write particular *words*, behind which enlightened readers could discern the (unrelated) messages from God.

However, if Christ is our center and if, as he says in John 5, the Scriptures are about him, we ought to be reading all of Scripture with Christ and the gospel in mind. How does this work? What does it mean (and what does it *not* mean) to read the Bible from the perspective of Christ and his gospel?

Jesus' teaching that the Scriptures are *about him* has led some interpreters to understand the Old Testament as having Christ encoded in each passage. They try to look between the lines of every text in order to discern what role Jesus has in it. This often leads to banal, repetitive, or fanciful Christianizations of the Old Testament.

For example, the book of Judges concerns Israel's failing leadership, and each section presents an increasingly hopeless picture of the nation's faithfulness. Where does one find Christ in this? He is obviously Israel's true and faithful leader, and under his command, the church will not fail. This is a wonderful and true message, but there are six main judges (Judg 3–16) and five more chapters as an epilogue detailing the lostness of the nation and its leaders (Judg 17–21). One could preach nineteen chapters of the book and make the same point (that Jesus is the true savior and king) each time. Preaching it as being literally *about Jesus* serves to turn a visceral and intriguing book into a monotone promotion of Jesus' divine leadership—something that no one is likely to have been confused about in the first place.

According to Paul's famous statement about Scripture in 2 Tim 2, it is not that the Old Testament is a non-stop allegory for Jesus' person and work. Rather, the Old Testament tells a story that has no ending, no resolution of the problem of sin and death at its heart, no release of the nation from spiritual exile and foreign occupation—all it leaves us with is threads of hope that God will act decisively to bring restoration and freedom. It is in this sense that the Old Testament is about Jesus—he comes as the resounding answer to all its open questions.

Reading the Bible as being about Jesus does not commit us to force-fit Jesus into texts or to proof-text our Christology from as many biblical sources as possible. Neither does it mean that each text is equally important to the gospel—some texts are more central than others. It means that we need the whole Bible to gain a fully-fledged understanding of God, ourselves, and the gospel. The Bible is there to tell us who Jesus is and what he came to do—we need the Old Testament to make sense of Christ, and Christ to provide the answer to it.

Reading Christ does not give us the power to *filter out* of God's word every text that we don't want to be part of the gospel message—as if it is only the parts that we think are about Jesus that are important. But neither does any of us argue that every verse of the Bible is as important as the next. Reading Christ does help us to know what Scriptural issues are worth fighting for.

The Christ-centered approach acknowledges that the stated purpose of God's revelation is for us to know God and Christ whom he has sent. To borrow Rick Warren's catch-phrase, our reading should be purpose-driven. The core gospel message is clear in Scripture because it is what Scripture is *about*—it is the climax of its storyline, it is repeated often, and it is filled in from multiple angles. There are a great many issues that are unclear in Scripture because God's purpose was not to resolve all open questions.

Christ-centered reading of Scripture helps us to deal with indeterminacy without having to fake certainty, or to make ourselves the only true interpreters, or to call all dissenters compromised. Christ-centered reading of Scripture avoids letting interpretation slip into chaos (as if everything were equally unclear or ambiguous), or extreme subjectivity (as if we are able to make ourselves and our interpretations the measure of its truth).

## The Gospel and Biblical Indeterminacy

Interpretive over-confidence and hostility towards outsiders are two common features of modern conservative evangelicalism, and both of these characteristics have a tendency to elevate secondary matters to the status of primary.

For example, as I have already argued, suspicion of evolutionists seems to me to have led many Christians to insist that creationism is essential to the faith. They tend to argue that the creation story teaches important theological principles (such as the intrusion of sin under the old Adam) on which the gospel relies. However, it is not *creationist* exegesis that identifies these principles as important; they are clearly a part of non-creationistic interpretations too. One doesn't have to throw out the baby when one throws out creationist bathwater.

Or take the story that I recently heard about a British theologian who applied for a job at a certain American seminary. He was asked which view of the Millennium he holds to and he replied that it is not an issue that has much traction in the UK and so he has no strong opinion on the matter. Unfortunately, not being a convinced premillennialist was a deal-breaker for the seminary and his application was declined. The Millennium is mentioned in one verse in the Bible.

If we agree that Christ and the gospel should be our center and that the core message should determine what issues are clear and necessary, and what issues are rightly unclear and unimportant, how do we practice it? What should our approach be to our true-but-open Scriptures?

Given that over-confidence makes us prone to promoting our own pet issues to a level of importance that they don't deserve, I suggest that the Bible's frequent indeterminacy on the one hand, and the commitment to Christ-centered reading of Scripture on the other, implies the following interpretive principle:

*We should express certainty in interpretation only to the degree that the evidence allows certainty, and we should express flexibility to the degree that the evidence produces indeterminacy.*

It is a problem that evangelicals teach such variety in doctrine when that variety is caused by irresponsible exegetical methods, but it is *right* for us to promote variety when the text itself leaves a matter open or gives us too little information to be certain.

## Disagreement over Disputable Matters

We are explicitly told not to let our Christian family be divided by those issues that are "disputable matters" or "matters of opinion" (Rom 14:1), and yet so many acrimonious church splits have taken place over issues that matter very little in the big scheme of things. Those of us who are committed to a high view of Scripture and to full obedience to its instructions should appreciate again what Paul teaches:

> "As for the one who is weak in faith, welcome him, *but not to quarrel over opinions* . . . Who are you to pass judgment on the servant of another? It is *before his own master that he stands or falls*. And he will be upheld, for the Lord is able to make him stand. One person esteems one day as better than another, while another esteems all days alike. *Each one should be fully convinced in his own mind.* The one who observes the day, observes it in *honor of the Lord* . . . Why do you pass judgment on your brother? Or you, why do you despise your brother? For we will all stand before the judgment seat of God . . . So then each of us will give an account of himself to God. Therefore let us not pass judgment on one another any longer, but rather *decide never to put a stumbling block or hindrance in the way of a brother.* I know and am persuaded in the Lord Jesus that nothing is unclean in itself, but it is unclean for anyone who

thinks it unclean. For if your brother is grieved by what you eat, *you are no longer walking in love.* By what you eat, do not destroy the one for whom Christ died. *So do not let what you regard as good be spoken of as evil.* For the kingdom of God is not a matter of eating and drinking but of righteousness and peace and joy in the Holy Spirit. Whoever thus serves Christ is acceptable to God and approved by men. So then let us *pursue what makes for peace and for mutual upbuilding.*" (Rom 14:1, 4-6, 10, 12-19)

In this text, Paul discusses those who can be regarded as "weak"—in this case because they felt constrained to avoid "unclean" meat or to observe certain holy days.[2] His instruction is as follows:

- Welcome them in, but not in order to *fix* them.
- We are not to judge others on matters of opinion; God will decide how to evaluate the service of his servants; the other servants don't have a say.
- There is a place for conviction and certainty. You are free in faith to commit fully to your opinion and to exercise it in honor of God, but you are not free to force your certainty on others.
- Judging others over secondary issues puts stumbling blocks in their way, and this destructive behavior *is* a core issue! It is the antithesis of walking in love, and the "good thing" that you are trying to impress on others becomes an *evil* thing in the eyes of those who witness the destruction.
- We don't pursue our own rightness as Christians—we honor God, not ourselves. Rather, we pursue whatever "makes for peace and mutual upbuilding."

So then, being fully persuaded of something that isn't core and that involves opinion (as Paul was about "unclean" food) is perfectly good, but it is *between you and God*. The good and evil that God *will* bring under judgement is not whose theology is best, but rather who showed love, protected the faith of the other, and pursued peace and mutual edification. Pursuing *mutual* edification is itself an acknowledgement from the apostle that we are all growing and in need of the other. We aren't ever the finished article.

---

2. I have heard alternate explanations of who is the weak and the strong in this text, but for our purposes, the specifics are not especially important.

## Judging between Core and Secondary Matters

Paul tells us to pass on the pattern of sound teaching and to defend against false teaching. But he also tells us to keep our opinions in check and not to get into fruitless arguments. If we are to obey Scripture, it is essential that we are able to distinguish between what is to be defended and what can be left to each person's own convictions.

While many people like to see things in black-and-white with as little grey as possible in between, I suggest that we view certainty of interpretation as a circle that fades by degree towards the edges:

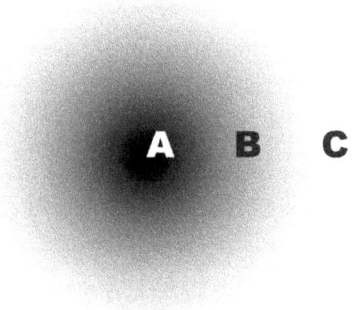

There are some things that have a high degree of certainty and are close to the center (A); there are some that have good but inconclusive evidence and are in grey areas (B); and there are some that are so doubtful, peripheral, or unclear that they are barely in the circle (C).

Issues such as the bodily resurrection of Christ are clear 'A' issues, because the resurrection is at the very heart of the gospel, there is no doubt that the writers of the New Testament understood it as historical and bodily, and, for a not-to-be-repeated miracle, there is an excellent historical argument that something earth-shattering really happened. It is undoubtedly the event at the center of evangelical Christianity.

'B' issues would include questions such as what baptism means and how we should practice it, or whether or not Samson should be regarded as a good guy or a bad guy. In each case, there is a good-sized body of relevant evidence, but none of it yields a clear verdict, and as long as one's beliefs are not accompanied by other anti-gospel teaching (such as that one's baptism grants salvation) there is nothing essential that rests on the decision one way or the other.

'C' issues are those about which the Bible says very little, and about which we are forced to speculate. They might be matters of preference—such as whether we may only use certain musical instruments in church but not others—or matters of theology that have far too little attestation. The Millennium in Revelation is an example of these. There is only one verse that mentions it (though there is more material that is of relevance to the issue), and how one views it depends heavily on whether you consider Revelation to be structured as a series of cycles or describing a linear sequence of events at the end of time. Furthermore, the Millennium has almost no bearing on the gospel—even if one never read Revelation, there are enough passages that encourage us to keep persevering and that urge us to be ready to meet Christ at all times. If he returns and rules for a thousand years or returns and brings everything to a close at once, the responsibility remains the same. Christians who are strongly convinced of their view and those who have no opinion at all seem to still have the same gospel and same way of life. It's a meaningless fight.

Therefore, the questions that we might ask in order to decide between central issues and peripheral ones include:

- How frequently does this issue get reiterated in the Bible? Is there a lot of evidence or a little?

- How clearly does the Bible present its perspective(s) on the matter? Is clarity diluted by the genre or literary techniques used? Do interpreters differ strongly, and if so, why?

- How consistent is the Bible's viewpoint on the matter? Is there counter-evidence? Does it comport with larger trajectories of biblical thought (such as the Christian worldview or ethos)?

- How directly does this issue relate to or impact the gospel? What is at stake?

To show how this might function, consider the examples of ordaining women and ordaining people in homosexual relationships. It is often argued that if one "gives ground" on the matter of ordaining women, by the "same hermeneutic" we will also have to approve of the ordination of practicing homosexuals too. I agree that the hermeneutical method can be seen as the same, but the result of applying the hermeneutic *isn't*. Consider how the answers to the questions above differ in each case:

|  | Ordaining Women | Ordaining Homosexuals |
|---|---|---|
| *Direct evidence:* | 1 Tim 2; Titus 1:6 (if the male language is limiting and not conventional). | Lev 18, 20;[3] Rom 1; 1 Cor 6; 1 Tim 1; Jude's reflection on Sodom. |
| *Indirect evidence:* | Submission of wives to husbands is endorsed more than once; Paul can be seen to be saying that male primacy is part of creation order.[4] | The indirect evidence is mostly negative—adultery and sexual immorality prohibit all non-marital sex; gay marriage seems to have been unknown. |
| *Clarity:* | Low—1 Tim. 2 uses unique terminology (e.g., for "authority"); contextually, women were identified as being a "way in" for false teachers in that particular church; Ephesus was known for its goddess cult that may have influenced the position of women in that church. | Moderate to high—while some argue that the terminology might refer to sexual *abuses*, not all forms of homosexuality, Leviticus is general, and Rom 1 speaks about male *and* female homosexuality, not male abuse of boys. It may have been prohibited due to Paul wanting Christians to avoid association of the gospel with a cultural stigma in that era, but it's not likely. |
| *Consistency (counter-evidence):* | Low—there are authoritative women: female prophets, judges, and "wise men"; Paul names several female "co-laborers in the gospel"; Junia is called an apostle; Priscilla was a teacher of Apollos and courier of the letter of Romans (a role that usually involved *explanation* of the letter); women are permitted to prophesy (ranked as second highest gift in 1 Cor. 12 and 14, and for edification of the church); Gal. 3 says: "there is neither male nor female." | High—there is no direct or indirect approval of homosexuality; there is no suggestion that sexual standards of morality have been or will be loosened in Christ. |
| *Gospel connection:* | None—if 1 Tim 2 were missing from our Bibles we would be unlikely to infer that such a command were needed, and having female teachers seems to make no obvious difference to any core aspect of the faith. | Moderate—moral issues have direct impact on Christian holiness and witness. If homosexuality were not specifically mentioned we *would* be likely to infer that it falls outside of the Bible's pattern for sex and marriage. |

*Evidence against ordaining women and homosexuals*

3. I include Leviticus in spite of the Old Testament law not being binding on Christians because it provides an instance of Old Testament agreement with New Testament teaching. The opposition to homosexuality is not limited to a specific era or occasion.

4. I personally disagree with this interpretation; when Paul invokes Eden in 1 Tim 2, he seems to me to be making an analogy in which, like Eve, these women are providing a conduit for temptation and falsehood, and exercising an inappropriate kind of authority.

You may quibble with my summary above, of course—these issues are much more complicated than what can be put in a page-long table. My point is that good hermeneutics requires us to consider cultural and contextual background, to consider direct and indirect evidence, and to take into account progressive revelation and biblical theology.

In this case, the apparent prohibition of women teaching men is based on a small number of texts, there are many examples that would seem to imply women in authority and/or teaching ministries, and there is nothing clearly of gospel importance that hinges on it. It is a matter that sits somewhere on the faded edges of the fuzzy-circle diagram.

The ordination of practicing homosexuals, however, is based on a few direct texts and many indirect texts (about sexuality in general). Although one's sexuality does not directly threaten the gospel message, moral responsibility is very important to biblical Christianity as part of holiness and one's witness to the truth of the gospel. Crucially, there is no hint of approval of homosexual practice in the Bible, and the qualifications for ordination imply a *higher* demand for exemplary conduct than non-ordinands. For these reasons, the biblical teaching about homosexuality seems to me much closer to an 'A' issue.

In short, "giving ground" on the issue of women in ministry does not set a precedent for the ordination of those whom the Bible calls sexually immoral. On the contrary, applying the same hermeneutic results in a mixed and indefinite verdict for the former (such that ordaining women or refusing to do so both have biblical support), but it results in unmixed disapproval of the latter.[5]

Because of the levels of uncertainty regarding the Bible's teaching on women in ministry, we should express a commensurate degree of doubt in our teaching about it. Of course it is necessary to decide on one practice or another, but this should be accompanied by humility and friendship towards those whose practices differ.

---

"Eve was deceived first" doesn't mean that women are easily deceived, because the false teachers themselves are clearly male! Men in Ephesus are already deceived and deceiving.

5. For what it is worth, homosexuality seems to me to involve matters of genetics, upbringing, identity, psychology, and sexual attraction. It is extraordinarily complex and not usually something that is idly chosen or easily changed. In saying that the Bible is only opposed to it, I do not mean to imply that it is right for anyone to express personal hostility to homosexual people, nor that they should be made unwelcome in churches. The point is merely that the Bible seems to define it as sexual sin, and so it should be dealt with as we deal with all sins—pastorally and with love.

Because the Bible's teaching is clearer on the matter of homosexuality, it is right that we express greater certainty in our presentation of that teaching. Some churches may choose to approve of homosexuality anyway, but it is relatively clear that this is done in spite of biblical teaching, not because of it. Of course we should always *listen* to those who disagree with us in case we have missed a crucial factor or misinterpreted a text, but we have a responsibility to promote the Bible's standard of Christian discipleship (even when it is unpopular) and to call such churches back to obedience to Scripture.

## Disagreement over Core Issues

While reading Christ might help to solve problems related to peripheral issues, what about disagreement over matters that are central to the faith—for example, the "New Perspective on Paul" has questioned whether Christians have properly understood *justification and works of law*. These are hardly matters of little consequence.

We should recognize, however, that there is still (among those with evangelical commitments to the truth and authority of Scripture) agreement about the core principles of the doctrine and its general contours. We agree on the *need* for justification in Christ, and that the Bible teaches that justification comes as a gift from God and precludes human boasting (e.g., Eph 2:9). In other words, the uncertainty over justification concerns *aspects* of the doctrine, not the doctrine as a whole.

Secondly, and perhaps more importantly, human knowledge is never fully formed. There are some famous examples from history in which people arrived at the conclusion that final answers had been reached on a certain matter, only to be proven wrong. For centuries, Newton's laws of physics were considered to be *the* description of the inner workings of the universe—until Einstein improved upon them. The biological description of swans necessarily included that they are *white* birds, because European swans are white—until Europeans sailed to Australia, the territorial equivalent of Opposite Day, and found black ones.

We sometimes think that the proximity of the early church to Christ and the apostles means that they must have had pure and complete knowledge of Christian theology. However, reading early theologians can be eye-opening. In the New Testament itself, we read of the apostolic-era dispute over whether Gentiles needed first to become Jewish in order to be

Christian. In the early church, the first opponent of infant baptism known to us was an apologist called Tertullian, but, rather than reflecting true, uncorrupted baptismal practices, he opposed infant baptism because why would one waste a get-out-of-damnation-free card on an innocent infant? Rather delay it so that there is less chance of sinning mortally after it has been administered.[6]

Human knowledge is something that has to grow and develop—even the most central doctrines of our faith (Trinity, for example) needed to be understood and worked through over time. Even if we exclude individual interpreters' irrationality, ignorance, or corruption from the picture, some doubt and diversity in *every* doctrine is to be expected because most of them have a lot of moving parts, and there is no reason to expect that every aspect our doctrines is perfectly known and complete.

Christ-centered reading of Scripture should serve to point out that there is golden cord running through Scripture about which we *can* have clarity and unity, and which provides an overall purpose and context for more peripheral issues. Founding our evangelicalism on this as our center provides a basis for greater unity that outweighs peripheral matters of diversity that too often divide us.

---

6. Bridge and Phypers, *Water That Divides*, 55.

CHAPTER 7

## Faith, Hope, and Love

*But you are not in darkness, brothers and sisters, for that day to surprise you like a thief. For you are all children of light, children of the day. We are not of the night or of the darkness . . . But since we belong to the day, let us be sober, having put on the breastplate of faith and love, and for a helmet the hope of salvation. God has not destined us for wrath, but to obtain salvation through our Lord Jesus Christ, who died for us so that whether we are awake or asleep we might live with him. Therefore encourage one another and build one another up, just as you are doing. (1 Thess 5:4–5, 8–11)*

LIBERAL THEOLOGIANS OF THE twentieth century tried to "modernize" Christianity by stripping it of its pre-modern supernaturalism (such as miracles or God speaking from burning bushes), and attempting to free Jesus from all the legends in which the writers of the New Testament had supposedly bound him. However, once they had stripped all of that away, what was left for them to preach? The answer to that question was to see Christianity as a vision of a better world—God's kingdom now—in which justice reigns. The "gospel" for such communities became social action on behalf of the poor and oppressed.

For evangelicals on the other hand, this gospel was no gospel at all, because without the risen Christ, the kingdom built in this life may as well not have had God in it at all. The reaction to the threat of this liberal teaching was to emphasize the gospel as *hope in life beyond death* with God for eternity, and, crucially, to exclude Christian social action from having a part in the gospel message. Of course, it wasn't as if Christians *shouldn't* be doing good to those around them, but it shouldn't be called a part of the gospel. R. C. Sproul writes:

> "Many evangelicals at this period in history, in order to preserve the central significance of the proclamation of the gospel of Jesus Christ, gave renewed emphasis to evangelism. In many cases, this emphasis upon evangelism was done to the exclusion of the other pole of biblical concern, namely, mercy ministry to those who were poor, afflicted, and suffering. So glaring was the dichotomy between liberal and evangelical concerns that, sadly, many evangelicals began to distance themselves from any involvement in mercy ministries, lest their activities be construed as a surrender to liberalism."[1]

It is a sad feature of evangelical responses to threat that, rather than clinging more firmly to the fullness of the gospel, we have a tendency to swing in the other direction. It is as if the gospel is a pair of scales, and if a group puts too much weight on one side, to keep the gospel in balance we must over-weight the other side. In reality, of course, the gospel is not a pair of scales, and overbalancing makes a mess of the gospel, no matter which way you fall.

As we discussed in the previous chapter, the gospel is a multifaceted thing—it is the answer to the problem of sin and death, the problem that alienates us from the presence of God. Through the life, death, and resurrection of Jesus and the gift of the Holy Spirit, we are given life to the full and adopted into God's family and his kingdom. The gospel is not only what justifies us; it is also our calling. As Phil 2:12–13 says, our salvation is something to be *worked*, and God's work is to produce in us a will aligned to his and works that correspond to it. Is it in the next life that our will and works need to be shaped or in this one?

R. C. Sproul continues:

> "Even a cursory reading of the New Testament, however, makes it clear that the concerns of Jesus and of the New Testament writers cannot be reduced to an either/or dilemma . . . The choice that the church has is never between personal salvation and mercy ministry. It is rather a both/and proposition. Neither pole can be properly swallowed by the other. To reduce Christianity either to a

---

1. Sproul, *Do we believe the whole gospel?*

program of social welfare or to a program of personal redemption results in a truncated gospel that is a profound distortion."[2]

In John 13, Jesus gives a demonstration of the extent of his love—love that would soon be fully laid bare on the cross—and an example for us to follow (13:14–15). He washes his disciples' feet. Jesus claims to have washed his disciples clean—his redemptive work is restorative of the individual—but by also washing their feet, he leaves a cleansing mission for his disciples too. The gospel does not end with the holiness of the individual; it is tied up with—and validated by—an ethos of love and service of others. Jesus gives us a "new commandment"—we must love just as he has loved us, and through this love all people will know that we truly are his disciples (13:34–35). The gospel must be *lived out* or it is no gospel at all.

Faith is the response to the gospel that gifts us entry into God's saving grace in Christ. However, faith as a response to the Truth also commits us to being *agents of truth* too—we are children of the light, not the darkness.

Hope is the quality that fuels our perseverance in the gospel—we look ahead to the great reward of life in God's presence and the end of sin and death. However, hope is not something that suspends us until the kingdom comes—it is something that causes us to imitate God and to model the kingdom even as we wait.

Love—the greatest of the three—is the only quality that will fully make the transition from this life to the next. It is our ultimate modeling of God's character in the present. It prompts us to give service, to work for gospel unity, and ultimately to see that the objects of our love make the transition with us to the life to come. Love spreads the gospel.

In the next chapters, we will discuss what the gospel center, and the ethos of faith, hope, and love, mean for the Christian life.

---

2. Sproul, *Do we believe the whole gospel?*

CHAPTER 8

# Faith

*Then Pilate said to him, "So you are a king?" Jesus answered, "You say that I am a king. For this purpose I was born and for this purpose I have come into the world—to bear witness to the truth. Everyone who is of the truth listens to my voice." Pilate said to him, "What is truth?" (John 18:37–38)*

As is often observed, faith is not primarily the quality of unwavering assurance of something (whether it's God's existence or a desired answer to prayer). It is true that Jas 1:5–8, for example, tells his reader not to ask God in doubt and double-mindedness, or else they will receive nothing from the Lord. But in James, a double-minded person is someone who *doesn't walk the walk*, not someone who is unsure.[1] The same James points out that some of the most unwavering believers in the existence of the true God are not Christians at all:

> "You believe[2] that God is one; you do well. Even the demons believe—and shudder!" (Jas 2:19)

If even many of God's *enemies* believe fully that God is there, the kind of faith that matters is not so much "strong belief" as it is the quality of

---

1. Assuming that this is the same James who is said to be an apostle to the Jews (Gal 2:9), we should also be aware that he might have in mind a specific kind of double-mindedness particular to his Jewish audience—perhaps concerning doubts about whether Jesus is the Messiah, or inability to choose between the Christian way and Judaism.
2. "To have faith" and "to believe" are the same word in Greek.

*faithfulness*. What the double-minded person does not possess is consistent trust in and devotion to God. They say they trust God, but they live in a way that does not match their claim. This kind of doubt—the one that expresses itself in duplicity and hypocrisy—is anti-Christian.

The kind of faith that is lived out in the "life of faith" is not blind; it is not wishful thinking; it is not expressed in pretending to have an immediate face-to-face relationship with God (such that one hears God speaking out loud or receives one miracle after another). This faith is based on—and steadied by—the core of the gospel: Christ's life, death, resurrection, and kingdom. True faith trusts that God is good and at work, even when God seems most silent; it commits to faithful love and service of God and others, even though we perceive him and his work only as if "in a mirror dimly" (1 Cor 13:12).

The kind of doubt that expresses lack of certainty, or that questions what it hears, or that finds it hard to be joyful in times of difficulty—this doubt is not anti-Christian. It is an important *counterpart* of true faith.

## Faith and Doubt

Certainty is over-rated. Certainty is the bedfellow of the kind of faith that emphasizes the *quantity* of belief—the one that is so sure and unmixed that God *has to* act in honor of it. I don't see in Scripture any hint that God finds this show of human religious strength to be all that valuable. The kind of faith that God in Scripture labors to produce in his people—that of loyalty and trust—*opposes* certainty.

We don't have to express faithfulness and trust when there is certainty, only when there is *reason to doubt*. Take Adam, for example. In the Garden of Eden, Adam was unable to be faithful to Eve. It's not that he was *un*faithful; he just had no opportunity to cheat. Faithfulness and trust are only meaningful concepts when there is a realistic possibility of choosing betrayal. If you feel like giving up, or if you feel like this whole Christian thing might be a hoax, or if you feel that God's definitions of sin are unfairly denying you something good, you are experiencing necessary doubt—you are experiencing the possibility of choosing betrayal, which in turn gives you the opportunity to choose against your feelings and in favor of the truth you came to know and trust. It is an opportunity to express genuine Christian faith. In this way, doubt can be good.

A second reason why doubt can be good is that certainty produces stasis—the "don't fix what ain't broke" mentality—but a quality such as doubt is required for change. There needs to be dissatisfaction with the status quo and questioning of it if it is ever to be changed. And change is essential to the evangelical faith if we are to gain deeper apprehension of the truth and to realign ourselves to it—to be reformed and always reforming.

Perhaps the defining characteristic of evangelicalism is that we do not submit finally to the authority of human mediators (such as priests or popes or pastors), nor to traditions (such as councils or denominations), nor to personal experience (such as conscience, emotions, visions, or dreams), nor to reason (such that *we* are the measure of truth and right). Our final authority is God's Word—the gospel center—and the word of God expressed in Scripture.

Put like this it might seem that faith in God's word requires us to be *certain* about the Scriptures, not to live in doubt about what we read. Yet this is again to confuse Scripture with our *interpretations* of it. We are all fond of pointing out how often Christians in the past or those in the denomination across town have "got it wrong," but those interpreters were most likely just as sure of themselves as we are. You can be as certain in your interpretation of God's word as you like, but it hasn't prevented all of your forefathers from making a litany of errors. Your certainty that your views are "biblical" is likely to cause you to confuse God's word with your words about God's word. Certainty is likely to convince you that you have no need to look deeper or to listen to others or to change.

In short, evangelical submission to the authority of Scripture means that we trust God's word, but we *doubt ourselves* as interpreters. Evangelical scholars who are involved in the study of hermeneutics often describe this self-doubt as the "hermeneutic of suspicion." Anthony Thiselton, for example, claims that hermeneutics should help us to read differently—to hear the text before we rush to our assumptions and expectations, to read with critical suspicion, "knowing how easy it is to be seduced into self-deception by self-interest."[3] In other words, it is a necessary component to interpretation that we are able to take a step back and ask to what degree we're reading our own contexts, interests, and preferences into the text.

More than this, it should make us aware that self-interest is not only *conscious* promotion of our own concerns. By virtue of our time in history, the place where we live, our race and gender, our upbringing, etc., we all

---

3. Thiselton, *Hermeneutics*, 5.

possess structures of thought and personal blind-spots that we're not aware of and that unconsciously motivate us to read in a certain way—often in a way that is completely alien to how an ancient interpreter would have read it. The hermeneutic of suspicion prompts us to be suspicious of our own interpretation, which in turn *should* prompt us to listen to those who have different assumptions, blind-spots, and gifts to ours. Neither of us is likely to be fully correct, but together we'll mitigate one another's weaknesses. But not if we're *certain* that we're right and they're wrong.

Thirdly, doubt is a cure for idolatry. This again might seem counter-intuitive—surely the person who is sold-out for Jesus and fully certain of what they believe is least likely to hold idolatries? Yes and no. I have already said that we should distinguish between double-mindedness and legitimate doubt. It is possible to be fully certain of who Jesus is and what he came to do, and yet still idolize one's family or reputation. On the other hand, one can fully believe and trust Christ and be entirely unsure of yourself or find yourself regularly questioning the basis of your faith.

The key element of idolatry is not false gods. What all idolatry shares in common is the attempt to grasp control of the uncontrollable. The New Testament has no interest in Baal or Asherah or Dagon or anyone else. The false god that the New Testament repeatedly identifies by name is *money*. Unlike Baal, money is a necessity for life in the world—Christians aren't told not to use money. However, like Baal, money is about controlling chaotic forces. Baal fought the capricious sea god who might withhold rain from the land, and so he was responsible for the fertility and prosperity of one's fields. Money, if you have enough of it, allows you to buy security, health, pleasure, and even *justice* (if you know which wheels to grease). Money becomes an idol when it gives us captaincy of our own ship and reduces the need for trust in God. This is also why the Bible identifies pride (1 Sam 15:23) and greed (Col 3:5) as forms of idolatry. Idolatry is ultimately about putting *ourselves* at the center.

While certainty feeds idolatries of arrogance and control, the useful forms of doubt cut against them. Without certainty, one can only trust. With doubt in oneself, one recognizes the chaos and one's inability to control it, and one must choose either despair or humility. Despair is the rebel's final stab at God. Humility is the posture of faith and reliance.

## Truth over Party

Faith is a commitment to trust God and submit oneself to his word and his will—to set aside one's own interests and to serve the interests of God and his creatures. An essential component of submission to God's word and his will is the recognition that God is a God of truth and that we are subject to what is true. Truth calls us to submit to a measure outside of ourselves and our own desires. Sin crafts truths of its own:

> "Woe to those who call evil good and good evil, who put darkness for light and light for darkness, who put bitter for sweet and sweet for bitter!" (Isa 5:20)

The trouble with culture war and the theological and political polarization that it produces is that culture warriors are by definition committed to their group's interests. You might object that your faction is fighting *for the truth*, but the other side believes that too. What ends up happening in practice is that the dictum: "All is fair in love and war" takes over and it becomes more important that your side wins.

A recent survey conducted by an organization called More in Common aimed to better understand polarization in America and to gain more detailed descriptions of American thought-worlds than the blunt binary of conservative or liberal. They describe their approach as follows:

> "The Hidden Tribes of America survey collected the views of more than 8,000 people, a group of US citizens statistically representative of the population based on census data. We also conducted six hour-long focus groups and 30 one-on-one interviews of at least one hour's duration with people from across the seven population segments . . . We also aimed to understand *why* people held the positions they did through a specially designed series of questions that helped us identify people's core beliefs about the world— questions about their identity and the basic values and beliefs that influence the way people see the world."[4]

The survey used the questions about core beliefs, identity, and values to identify the seven "hidden tribes." The two groups at either end of the spectrum they describe as "progressive activists" (8 percent of the population) and "devoted conservatives" (6 percent of the population). These are the people who are both strongly persuaded of their political stance and highly active in political life.

4. More in Common, *Hidden Tribes*.

In one group of questions, participants were asked to choose which they agreed with more, and the results were as follows:

## IMMIGRATION

A) Undocumented immigrants who arrived as children and have grown up here should be protected from deportation and given the chance to earn citizenship.

B) The government should be able to deport anyone living in America who doesn't have a legal right to be here.

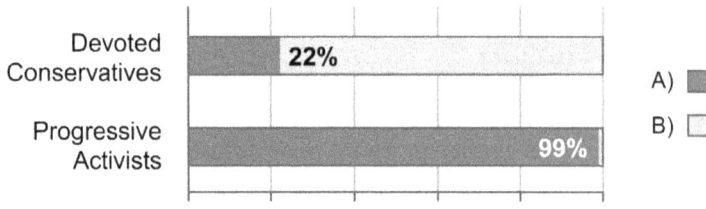

## DONALD TRUMP

A) I "slightly", "somewhat", or "strongly" disapprove of the way President Donald Trump is doing his job.

B) I "slightly", "somewhat", or "strongly" approve of the way President Donald Trump is doing his job.

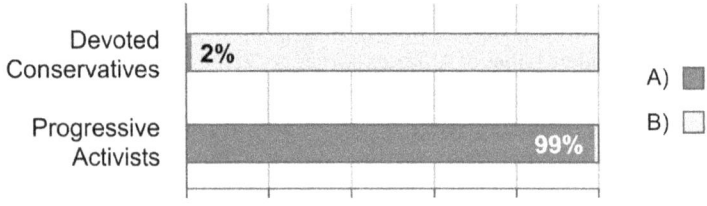

## FEMINISM

A) Today's feminists fight for important issues.
B) Today's feminists just attack men.

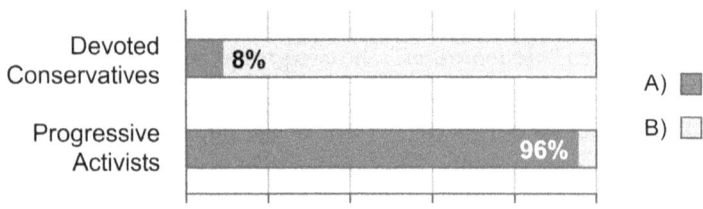

### POLICE

A) The police are often more violent towards African Americans than others.
B) The police are mostly fair towards people of every race.

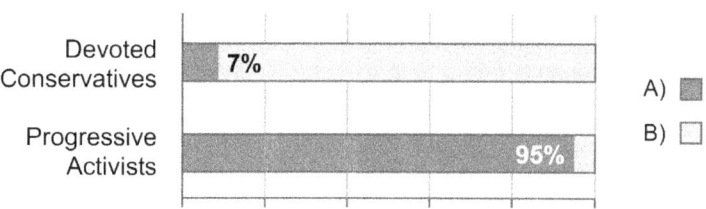

In another set of questions, the two groups were asked to what extent they agreed with certain statements. The following two examples are the most polarized of the results, but other results were not dissimilar.

### SUCCESS
"Hard work will always lead to success."

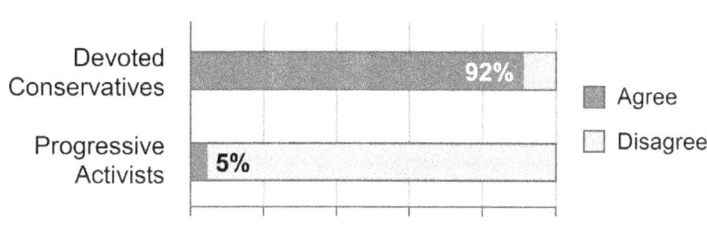

### WELFARE
"Government should take more responsibility to ensure everyone is provided for."

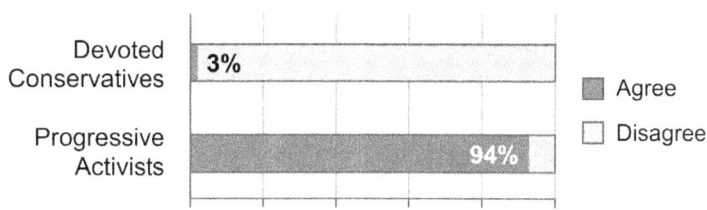

On one hand, it is not surprising that strongly conservative and liberal political views should be almost the total inverse of one another, but on the other hand, very few of these issues are *political*—they are matters of perception or ethics. There is nothing about one's opinion on racial bias and police brutality, for example, that is identifiably conservative or liberal or related to policy in any way. Or how is it possible that the question of whether someone is doing a good job or not—the kind of thing that the corporate world measures on a regular basis—could yield 99 percent disapproval from one group and 98 percent approval from the other? If job performance is measurable, then one's perception of how well the job is being performed should be related to the facts; individuals might prioritize certain things over others and come to a different conclusion, but why would this divide along party lines?

These results really *should* be a surprise, because they demonstrate the degree to which those who are deeply involved in the polarized political landscape have their opinions and values shaped largely or entirely by what *the party* needs at a given point in time. It is clear—and concerning—that these positions are not determined by evidence of what is right and wrong but almost entirely by tribal identity.

The implications of this for truth are obvious—in society at present, truth is considered to be unimportant, or worse, something subjective that is *chosen*, not actual. This in turn means that accountability is also not possible. If there is not a standard of truth to which even one's own tribe is held—if the important thing is merely to win or at least to save face—then there is no possibility of rooting out corruption. The bad behavior of leaders will always be subject to outrage from one team and defensiveness from their own. Guilt or otherwise becomes irrelevant.

Unfortunately, it is not the postmodern, God-hating liberals who deny the existence of truth and mold facts to fit a desired outcome (or at least not only them). It is the conservative politicians who are leading the way with "fake news" and "alternative facts," and far too many evangelical Christians are either vocally supportive of their political tribe, or at least silently complicit. The same Christians who argue that secular culture is corrupting the church (on matters of feminism, for example) seem unconcerned about the relativizing of truth in their own political camp—something that is undoubtedly secular and a serious threat to our claim to have a gospel that is true for everyone.

## Patterned Thinking and Confirmation Bias

A major reason why even Christians struggle to submit to truth, choosing rather to follow their feelings or their tribe or their traditions, is that humans are not first and foremost rational creatures. For the servicing of most of our basic needs and social relationships, our ability to recognize patterns is much more successful than having to rigorously test whether something is true. If we see an advancing line of black clouds, we'd best get inside because this usually means rain is coming. It might end up being a false assumption, but we'll stay dry either way. If we see an advancing line of smoke billowing from the forest ahead of us, perhaps we'd better turn around because smoke usually means fire, and waiting to make sure might kill us. If I were wearing red-white-and-blue socks when the USA soccer team won their last two games, then I'd better always wear those socks so that they can win more games.

As this last example illustrates, patterned thinking isn't rational—it's much closer to prejudice than reason. We behave according to patterns because they're fairly reliable and can be applied instantly and without having to rethink. The trouble is that relying on what amounts to prejudice is good for snap judgements and brute matters of survival, but it can often be very damaging in situations where care and insight are required. Truth and reason require *trained minds*. We have to *overcome* our patterned thinking if we are to judge rightly.

Prov 10:4 says:

> "A slack hand causes poverty, but the hand of the diligent makes rich."

This is a general rule—a pattern. There are, however, many exceptions: some lazy people are rich due to inheritance, good luck, or corruption. "The poor are poor because they are lazy" is not a rule at all—it is an irrational reversal of the order of this proverb and it leads to a cruel conclusion: the poor are to blame for their own poverty. Patterned thinking leads to bad judgement in cases that require truth and nuance.

Patterns can be fiendishly difficult to dislodge and they give us a false sense of mastery. This leads to over-confidence and unearned arrogance about what one thinks one knows. A study was conducted in which students were asked to evaluate data concerning the death penalty. The data was fictitious and it presented equally compelling evidence that the death penalty is a deterrent of crime and that it is *not* a deterrent. Students who began the study thinking that the death penalty is a deterrent rated the data that supported their belief very credible, and those who thought the opposite did the reverse. Kolbert adds that the confirmation provided by this fake data had an effect:

> "At the end of the experiment, the students were asked once again about their views. Those who'd started out pro-capital punishment were now even more in favor of it; those who'd opposed it were even more hostile."[5]

If we are not conscious of our own thinking and trained to be self-critical, we will usually welcome evidence that supports our beliefs and we will ignore evidence that opposes it. Without conscious, rational intervention in our thinking patterns, therefore, we will continue to see what we want to see. Preachers often warn congregations about those who only listen to what their "itching ears" want to hear, but *this is all of us*—the preacher included—unless we commit to unwiring our lazy patterned thinking and to pursuing truth.

In another study, conducted at Yale, students were asked to rate their understanding of how everyday things such as toilets and locks work. Next, they were asked to give a detailed *explanation* of how these things work and to rate their understanding again. The first rating indicated a high degree of confidence in their understanding, whereas once they were pushed to demonstrate it, they became more aware of their ignorance and their confidence dropped. They had *familiarity* with these things, not knowledge. Genuine understanding requires humility (because we can't learn if we're already satisfied with what we know) and the commitment to pursue the truth.[6]

Several studies have demonstrated that *ignorance and zeal* often go hand-in-hand. Socrates apparently said that the wisest of people are those who know that they don't know. A description of a cognitive bias that we're all prone to, known as the Dunning-Kruger effect, describes the converse of Socrates's idea: people tend to be ignorant of their own ignorance.[7]

The following graph illustrates how we perceive our own expertise, especially when it comes to non-technical things:[8]

5. Kolbert, *Facts*.
6. Kolbert, *Facts*.
7. Dunning, "Dunning-Kruger Effect."
8. No sane people over-estimate their ability to build their own mobile phone, for example, or to speak a foreign language. But when it comes to matters about which it is

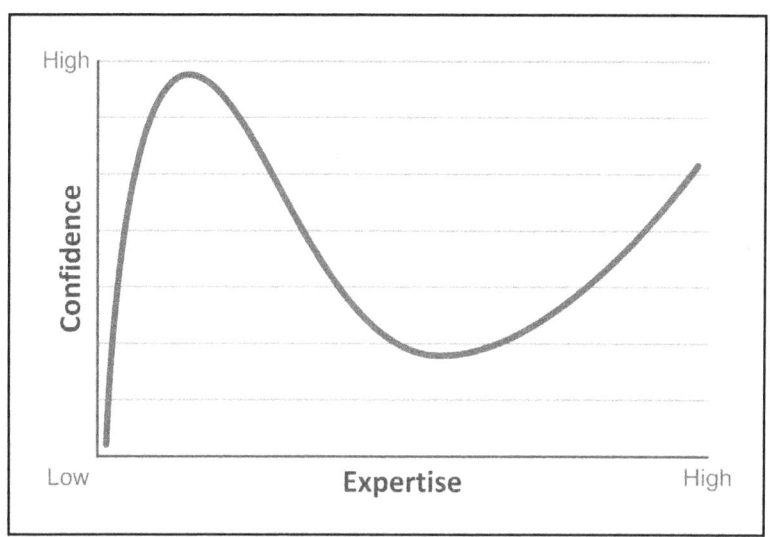

*The Dunning-Kruger Effect*

Dunning and Kruger found that people with only basic knowledge of a subject tend to massively overestimate what they know, and people with moderate expertise—those who know enough to know how little they know—tend to underestimate their ability. The people who are surest of themselves are either ignorant or masters of the field.

The take-home from all of this is that truth is very much under threat both from cognitive biases that are well known in research but vastly underappreciated by most of us, and from political and religious rhetoric that plays on them (whether intentionally or not). Strong beliefs and full confidence tend to be attributes of those who are arrogant, not those who possess full knowledge of the truth. Attempts to convince people that they have *misunderstood* the truth will be hampered by confirmation bias that filters out the evidence such people don't like, and even if their initial belief is proven to be unfounded, they may continue to hold it anyway, because beliefs are "perseverant."[9]

---

possible to form opinions, such as how to run the country, the Dunning-Kruger effect comes into play.

9. As we observed in chapter 2: "Once formed . . . impressions are remarkably perseverant." (Kolbert, *Facts*).

A case in point is the anti-vaccine movement, which was sparked by medical research that claimed that vaccines cause autism. The research was shown to be fraudulent, results have never been replicated elsewhere despite repeated efforts to do so, and the author was stripped of his medical license. Nevertheless, scores of people without a medical or research background and without evidence, and in spite of a weight of evidence to the contrary, continue to believe with vehemence that there is a big-pharma conspiracy behind it all, and they don't vaccinate their children as a result.

> "As a rule, strong feelings about issues do not emerge from deep understanding."[10]

If one of the defining characteristics of evangelicals is that we recognize Scripture as true and as our final authority, it ought to mean that we *answer to truth*. If we believe that *God is truth*, we have all the more responsibility as imitators of God to insist that truth matters. If evangelicals spend the week celebrating their political tribe's bespoke "truth" and they spend Sunday telling sinners: "Jesus is the way, the truth, and the life," on what grounds does our gospel have the least shred of credibility? Jesus becomes just another thing that is merely "true for you."

It is a matter of extreme urgency that evangelicals cut ties with the fruitless polarization of the political landscape and recover their center. It's not just that we are failing to be examples of Christlikeness to the watching world; it's that we're becoming examples of *what not to be*.

---

10. Sloman and Fernbach, quoted in Kolbert, *Facts*.

# Chapter 9

# Hope

*Therefore, my beloved, as you have always obeyed, so now, not only as in my presence but much more in my absence, work out your own salvation with fear and trembling, for it is God who works in you, both to will and to work for his good pleasure. (Phil 2:12–13)*

SOME YEARS AGO, A friend recommended to me John Piper's book *Future Grace*. In it, Piper repeatedly uses the catchphrase: "The purifying power of living by faith in future grace." As I was reading, I was skeptical about how much I could support what he was saying, because I wasn't sure what he meant. It took me until about page 150 to realize that he was talking about Christian *hope*.

Piper seems to have resisted immediately characterizing it as a book about hope because a) catchphrases are cool, and b) he presumably wanted us to look at hope with new eyes. It's not just a distant expectation of heaven after we die; it's about a relationship with the Living God whose gifts of grace are part of our expectation of our *entire* future—both tomorrow and into eternity. Recognizing the true nature of hope means living every day in a heavenly-minded way.

## Hope and Heavenly-Mindedness

Perhaps you have heard the clichéd criticism of pious Christians that they are "too heavenly-minded to be of earthly good." It seems to have largely gone out of circulation as a criticism, probably because there are much better insults and because Christians being too holy and too otherworldly is hardly the thing that outsiders find most annoying about us right now.

In any case, the criticism implies that Christian people who put their hope exclusively in the afterlife have surrendered any concern for the present world. Consequently, they have become hopeless as vessels for any meaningful change in this life.

C. S. Lewis answered this objection long ago in *Mere Christianity*. He wrote:

> "Hope is one of the theological virtues. This means that a continual looking forward to the eternal world is not (as some modern people think) a form of escapism or wishful thinking, but one of the things a Christian is meant to do. It does not mean that we are to leave the present world as it is. If you read history, you will find that the Christians who did most for the present world were just those who thought most of the next. The Apostles themselves, who set on foot the conversion of the Roman Empire, the great men who built up the Middle Ages, the English evangelicals who abolished the slave trade, all left their mark on earth, precisely because their minds were occupied with heaven. It is since Christians have largely ceased to think of the other world that they have become so ineffective in this. Aim at heaven and you will get earth 'thrown in'; aim at earth and you will get neither."[1]

When one locates Christian hope in a fully articulated Christian gospel—one that understands it as a movement from the loss of God's presence and into our restoration to full life with him—hope cannot merely be something for the life to come. It is true that the kingdom of God is presented as something that will fully come only at The End, but there are nevertheless many clues that our life now must be consistent with the kingdom living that we anticipate once all is finally fulfilled. Consider the following examples:

- In Luke 16, Jesus says:

    > "One who is faithful in a very little is also faithful in much, and one who is dishonest in a very little is also dishonest in much. If

---

1. Lewis, *Mere Christianity*, 135.

then you have not been faithful in the unrighteous wealth, who will entrust to you the true riches? And if you have not been faithful in that which is another's, who will give you that which is your own?" (Luke 16:10–12)

- In Luke 17:20–21, Jesus seems to depart from the kingdom only as a tangible restoration of Israel's dominion, and rather describes it as not coming in an observable way, but as something that "is in the midst of you."[2] It seems to suggest that kingdom transformation will take place though personal change, not national revolution.

- In Rom 14:17, Paul says: "For the kingdom of God is not a matter of eating and drinking but of righteousness and peace and joy in the Holy Spirit." Our lives here should reflect kingdom priorities.

- In 1 Cor 6:9, Paul points out that sinful living puts our inheritance at risk: "Or do you not know that the unrighteous will not inherit the kingdom of God?"[3]

- In Col 1:13, Paul speaks of the kingdom as a domain into which we have already been transferred: "He has delivered us from the domain of darkness and transferred us to the kingdom of his beloved Son."

- In 1 Thess 2:12, Paul exhorts his readers to, "walk in a manner worthy of God, who calls you into his own kingdom and glory." Our living must be consistent with our kingdom calling.

As Piper and Lewis both pointed out, our hope in God's kingdom—though it is finally revealed only at The End—nevertheless commits us to a life lived *now* in the pattern of that kingdom. True heavenly-mindedness means that we align our priorities according to the final destination.

If we understand hope only as in the next life, then we are in danger of surrendering this world and inviting unbelievers into an impoverished gospel. Jesus' invitation into the kingdom was not a repeat of Noah's Ark; he did not invite his people to abandon a sinking world and wait for the New Creation. On the contrary, he healed the sick, he gave sight to the blind, he supplied an over-abundance of good wine to a dying party, and he multiplied bread and fish for an impossible number of guests at his table.

---

2. I acknowledge that he is possibly claiming that the kingdom will arrive without warning and will appear suddenly among them.

3. See also Gal 5:21 and Eph 5:5.

Jesus came modeling his kingdom, and if we are likewise to model our future hope, far from it meaning lack of concern for the world, it will mean that we live as agents of restoration and reconciliation. Our gospel will not merely be the message of a lifeboat out of here. Our gospel will be visible in the way that we live and the way that we love, and it will be evident to outsiders that our gospel is good—they will see our good deeds and glorify God on the day of visitation (1 Pet 2:12). "For the kingdom of God is a matter of righteousness and peace and joy in the Holy Spirit."

## Hope and Justice

Evangelicals have always strongly believed that the gospel is not an intellectual acceptance of certain religious ideas, but something that must be *lived out*. Similarly, our hope in God's coming kingdom and Jesus' promise of life to the full are not focused only on eternity, but (at least in part) also in this life—life in God's kingdom is something that we model even now.

However, even though these are widely accepted ideas, many evangelicals continue to be suspicious of any groups that are excited about social projects or vocal in their opposition to injustice. The legacy of the evangelical reaction to the liberal "social gospel" is still with us.

### The Statement on Social Justice and the Gospel

In 2018, John MacArthur and a group of founding signatories produced a controversial document that makes a series of affirmations and denials concerning social justice. The *Statement on Social Justice and the Gospel* claims to be "for the sake of Christ and his church," and it styles itself as an urgent defense of Christianity against "dangerous ideas and corrupted moral values [that] will spread their influence into other realms of biblical doctrines and principles." They say:

> "We are deeply concerned that values borrowed from secular culture are currently undermining Scripture in the areas of race and ethnicity, manhood and womanhood, and human sexuality. The Bible's teaching on each of these subjects is being challenged under the broad and somewhat nebulous rubric of concern for 'social justice'."[4]

4. McArthur, *Statement on Social Justice*, Introduction.

Of course, some of the pressure coming from secular society does represent a threat to Christianity, and it remains as true as ever that we must be watchful. However, this document was met with criticism from many in the evangelical world too.

The most general criticisms include that:

- It decries the influence of secular culture on the church (as if social justice is merely cultural), but also fails to recognize its own cultural influences and preferences.
- Many of the issues covered in the document are extraordinarily complex, whereas the responses given to them are extraordinarily simplistic.
- Each statement is accompanied by a list of verses, but even the devil knows how to quote those. Why were certain texts chosen and not others? Does the full witness of Scripture lead to their conclusion or did their desired conclusion shape their selection of texts? Whose interpretation of the texts is being privileged? The stacking of Bible verses doesn't make that idea biblical.

Some of the specific entries serve as examples of why the above criticisms are important.

*"Feminist Pressure"*

The document includes a statement on sexuality and (oddly for their top fourteen statements relevant to justice) one on complementarianism. While there is much that is questionable about their claim that the Bible and biology assign men and women "distinct traits" and divide the sexes into "distinct roles" and that this somehow correlates to their "God-given gifts,"[5] the biggest problem with it is that it is clearly meant to be an example of where social (feminist) pressure is polluting the church. Yet non-complementarian evangelicals dissent on the basis of *exegesis*, not obeisance to liberal feminism, and many of the complementarianist definitions of women's

---

5. I don't deny that the sexes are different. Besides obvious physical differences, there are traits and gifts that tend to adhere more commonly to one sex than the other. However, these are *tendencies*, not universal, and the Bible makes no attempt whatsoever to define maleness and femaleness or to imply that gifts are in any way gendered. To insist on *distinct* male and female traits and gifts is dehumanizing to those whose God-given gifts and traits do not conform to a well-meaning pastor's idea of what they should be.

## Turn Neither Right Nor Left

traits, gifts, and roles align very well with "values borrowed from secular culture"—it's just culture from sixty years ago.

For example, noted Old Testament scholar Gerhard Von Rad, in his comments on Gen 3:6, wrote:

> "The one who has been led astray now becomes a temptress. That is meant to indicate that the woman confronts the obscure allurements and mysteries that beset our limited life more directly than the man does. In the history of Yahweh-religion it has always been the women who have shown an inclination for obscure astrological cults."[6]

This characterization of women did not raise eyebrows in the sixties when this book was first published, nor in the seventies when it was revised. It is not that Von Rad was a good complementarian who got women right. He was a theological liberal who was a man of his age—an age in which polite forms of sexism and racism were normal. As I have already observed, when Paul rebukes the "weak-willed women" of the Ephesian church for letting false teachers into their homes and churches (which is probably what he has in mind when he cites this part of Genesis), it is nevertheless *the men who are the false teachers*. The idea that women are easily fooled forgets that the men doing the fooling were themselves fooled first. It is a sexist characterization with which the last century was wrongly comfortable.

There might well be feminist cultural pressure that is damaging (just as there are damaging practices in most churches without it meaning that the churches as a whole are evil). However, "feminist pressure" exists because women—through much suffering and persecution—have finally been able to gain a platform from which they can address very real bigotry and oppression. It is remarkable that the church is slowest to address legitimate outcry against racial or sexist injustice, and quickest to denounce as suspect those who *do* respond to it.

In this case, the drafters of this document are very sure that those who view women in the church differently are doing so because they are slaves to the culture, but they're also entirely blind to their own secular-culture-inspired influences and preferences.

---

6. Von Rad, *Genesis*, 90.

## "Racial Pressure"

Several of the statements touch on issues of race, and most of the affirmations are general and agreeable. The denials that follow, however, tend to betray more of an agenda.

Statement V talks about sin, affirming that we are all alike condemned by it. No problems there. Yet the denial takes an odd turn, raising the connection of sin to *ethnicity*:

> "WE DENY that, other than the previously stated connection to Adam, any person is morally culpable for another person's sin. Although families, groups, and nations can sin collectively, and cultures can be predisposed to particular sins, *subsequent generations share the collective guilt of their ancestors only if they approve and embrace (or attempt to justify) those sins.* Before God each person must repent and confess his or her own sins in order to receive forgiveness. *We further deny that one's ethnicity establishes any necessary connection to any particular sin.*"[7]

Although this article acknowledges collective sins, there is a strong push to see moral responsibility as something that belongs only to individually chosen behavior, and not by our relatedness to and responsibility to one another. It is hard to see how anyone could be urged by this article to take responsibility to overturn unjust systems that were inherited from our forefathers, even though it is these systems that are most often identified as oppressive (racially or otherwise). Injustice is frequently communal; Christian justice can't be stubbornly individual.

The mention of ethnicity seems also to imply that sins of racism are in mind, and the talk of generational sin and guilt seems therefore to be about the culpability (or otherwise) of white people now for the sins of slavery and racial oppression perpetrated by their forefathers.

Statement XII is specifically about race. The denial reads:

> "WE DENY that Christians should segregate themselves into racial groups or regard racial identity above, or even equal to, their identity in Christ. We deny that any divisions between people groups (from an unstated attitude of superiority to *an overt spirit of resentment*) have any legitimate place in the fellowship of the redeemed. We reject any teaching that encourages racial groups to view themselves as privileged oppressors *or entitled victims of oppression.* While we are to weep with those who weep, we deny

---

7. McArthur, *Statement on Social Justice*, V.

> that a person's *feelings of offense or oppression necessarily prove that someone else is guilty of sinful behaviors, oppression, or prejudice.*"[8]

Superficially, there is little that is objectionable. If this were written into a context in which institutional racism had never been an issue and in which social fractures along racial lines did not exist, then there would be no reason to quibble with it. But because this *isn't* written into a neutral context, these statements come with a worrying subtext.

While they elsewhere acknowledge the possibility of *systemic* racism (statement XIV), the two statements quoted above effectively deny that white Americans bear any blame for current racial problems. Because individual white citizens did not themselves engage in or approve of slavery or racism, and as long as they themselves don't exhibit an attitude of superiority, they have no guilt and should not be criticized.

The first reason why these denials are unhelpful is that racism is extremely difficult to detect. In South Africa, a country run for decades by a nationalist-socialist party that wrote racism into law, it is almost impossible to find a white person who is or ever was racist—at least by their own reckoning. Racial tensions in our country are high because black South Africans are becoming frustrated by the slowness of change, and white South Africans (as a minority) are fearful of losing their wealth and position, and are thus strongly in denial about the need for change. So whites (a mere twenty-five years on from *Apartheid*) say exactly what this Social Justice statement says: *Apartheid* wasn't our idea; stop making us feel guilty. We're not racist; it was the National Party's fault. *Apartheid* is over; black people should stop playing the victim.

Systemic racism is not primarily about hate. It is about *trust*. Just as sexist men can marry and love women while still regarding them as inferior, racism should not be confused with hostility or ill-will towards other races. Racism need only be a small bias—a slight disparity in the degree to which you trust one race group over another—for it to have massive social impact. But these small disparities in trust pass through us unnoticed *even when we're looking for them.*[9] When you're encouraged—with a panel of Bible verses in support—to deny that it's a problem or to wag a finger at agitators, you're being told to look away. There is no hope that you'll find that you might be part of the problem.

---

8. McArthur, *Statement on Social Justice*, XII.
9. For more on this, please read Pickering, *Friendly Racism*.

The second reason why these denials are problematic is that they remove any responsibility of the individual to address racist institutions or systems. It is true that our forefathers were the colonialists and slave traders and Klan members that set up the prejudicial systems that created social division, not us. However, subsequent generations continue to benefit from or suffer because of those past sins. The problem exists now, and we are either part of the problem or active in dismantling it.

Furthermore, to deny that white people are privileged as a group and that black people are victimized as a group in American society is absurd. Of course any generalization about any group is likely to have individuals that are exceptions to the rule, but the rule exists nevertheless. Groups that hold power or privilege because of past sins are highly likely to deny that they do—because that would imply personal responsibility—and they are highly likely to continue acting in service of their own interests.

I recently was involved in a dispute regarding Donald Trump's commitment to look into farm murders taking place in South Africa. These murders happen, but they have been appropriated by white supremacist groups as evidence of "white genocide." These groups have inflated figures and obscured the degree to which the targets of these murders are very often black farmers too.

I pointed this out, with documentary evidence, along with the observation that whites remain radically privileged in South Africa—only 1 percent of whites live in poverty, compared with 60 percent of blacks who still do. A response from a woman who identified herself as "Prayerful Chick" and a lover of God and guns was:

> "They should get off their butts and work."

I have heard similar sentiments about poverty from at least one prominent televangelist.[10] The idea is that hard work leads to success, whereas poverty is due to laziness. I doubt that this bears up to a moment's scrutiny even in America, but in South Africa, blacks were prevented from holding professional positions and were mostly restricted to manual labor and positions of servants. The schools of black children received about 5 percent of the funding that white schools were given. Government infrastructure-investment in black "homelands" was minimal. The devastation that this caused to black participation in the economy was total and will not be undone

---

10. Given how little televangelism I watch, I imagine it is more prevalent than just one offender.

for decades to come. But being able to blame the poor for their poverty is an easy way to make sure that you feel very little obligation to affect any change or even to acknowledge the institutional privileges you and your forefathers enjoyed at the expense of the oppressed. It is, after all, your *hard work* that got you what you have.

Systems and institutions are impersonal; if you define blameworthiness as individual *only*—something unjust that a person consciously chooses—there is no possible way of addressing systemic injustice. But, individuals do not need to approve of or embrace personal sinful attitudes of racism in order to perpetuate a racist system.

Dr. Martin Luther King Jr. wrote about this decades ago—none of us should have any excuse for seeming confused about it. He said:

> "History is the long and tragic story of the fact that privileged groups seldom give up their privileges voluntarily. Individuals may see the moral light and voluntarily give up their unjust posture; but, as Reinhold Niebuhr has reminded us, *groups are more immoral than individuals*."[11]

This social-justice statement that takes side-swipes at those groups with a "spirit of resentment" or who are "entitled victims of oppression" or who too quickly develop "feelings of offense" ironically is exerting cultural pressure on the church to *ignore injustice*, rather than championing its end. The subtext underlying these statements seems to me to be akin to the sentiments of the "All lives matter" advocates. It's true in a neutral context but rotten to the core as a response to the American context today.

Christians, as agents of a just God, need to take systemic injustice more seriously. No one person is responsible for it and no one living in the system consciously chooses it, but we all keep it alive—and we are absolutely to blame for that. Choice implies an alternative, and the only way that an alternative to an unjust system is possible is if critical people imagine one and work to make it real. Christians should be at the forefront of affirming positive social change, not listing denials that enable them to wash their hands of the problem.

---

11. King, *Letter from Birmingham Jail*.

## "Social-activist Pressure"

The social-justice statement includes several points that deal directly with the authors' idea of justice.

The positive affirmations about justice (statement III) put the responsibility on the individual to imitate our just God by (surprisingly passively) living "justly in the world," which "includes showing appropriate respect to every person and giving to each one what he or she is due." The approach to systemic injustice puts the responsibility on "societies" to "establish laws to correct injustices."

This is hardly a manifesto for Christians as change agents.[12]

The denials underline that standards of justice should be derived from Scripture rather than variable, socially-constructed definitions. The statement concerning the gospel (statement VI) defines it as the "message concerning the person and work of Jesus Christ—especially his virgin birth, righteous life, substitutionary sacrifice, atoning death, and bodily resurrection" that promises salvation to whoever believes. The denial, however, says that nothing else can be added to this gospel message "without perverting it into another gospel" and they define justice as important but not a gospel issue.

The statement concerning the church (statement VII) adds:

> "WE DENY that political or social activism should be viewed as integral components of the gospel or primary to the mission of the church . . . we deny that these activities are either evidence of saving faith or constitute a central part of the church's mission."[13]

These statements about our gospel and mission are precisely the sort of thing that R. C. Sproul calls "a truncated gospel." It is not just Sproul either. The writer of the book of James doesn't merely call it truncated; he calls it *dead*. He says:

> "What good is it, my brothers, if someone says he has faith but does not have works? Can that faith save him? If a brother or sister is poorly clothed and lacking in daily food, and one of you says to them, 'Go in peace, be warmed and filled,' without giving them the things needed for the body, what good is that? So also faith by

---

12. It is also strange that—at least from an outsider's perspective—it is the liberal party that agitates for laws that aim at uplifting disadvantaged communities, whereas the conservative party (preferred by evangelicals) seems to work hard to dismantle them.

13. McArthur, *Statement on Social Justice*.

> itself, if it does not have works, is dead. But someone will say, 'You have faith and I have works.' Show me your faith apart from your works, and I will show you my faith by my works. You believe that God is one; you do well. Even the demons believe—and shudder!" (Jas 2:14–19)

In this passage, James says that faith is something that even demons have. What they don't have is the will to carry out the implications of the faith. Faith in a gospel that does not issue in actions—tellingly characterized as helping the poor in this case—is a dead faith.

You might object that "faith" is not the gospel message; it is our *response* to the gospel message, and so works are an appropriate response but not part of the gospel itself. James goes on:

> "Do you want to be shown, you foolish person, that faith apart from works is useless? Was not Abraham our father justified by works when he offered up his son Isaac on the altar? You see that faith was active along with his works, and faith was completed by his works; and the Scripture was fulfilled that says, 'Abraham believed God, and it was counted to him as righteousness'—and he was called a friend of God. *You see that a person is justified by works and not by faith alone.* And in the same way was not also Rahab the prostitute justified by works when she received the messengers and sent them out by another way? *For as the body apart from the spirit is dead, so also faith apart from works is dead.*" (Jas 2:20–26)

Here he says not merely that *faith* and works go together, but also *justification* and works. Abraham had to demonstrate his faith by his actions, and only when *faith and actions were in alignment*, says James, could his faith be credited as righteousness. He sums up by comparing faith to a dead body when it is separated from its spirit—works in alignment with the gospel give it life.

The social justice statement insists that faith in Christ's justifying work is the whole gospel and anything added to it is a distortion. Their statement on racism says about teaching[14] on social issues that "historically, such things tend to become distractions that inevitably lead to departures from the gospel." But James says that faith and works together are necessary components of righteousness by faith. A gospel message without *gospel*

---

14. In fact, they dismissively characterize teaching on social justice in the church as "lectures," as opposed to evangelism and exposition, which they call "preaching."

*living* was never alive in the first place. I imagine we would agree that a dead gospel is not complete, and that adding the thing that brings it to life is not a distortion but a necessity. Leaving the gospel at the saving work of Christ is a truncated gospel that *leaves out* what makes it good news.

It is strange that a document purporting to protect the church from dangerous teaching and to present a biblical view of justice should imply that feminists who are working to uncover abuse and discrimination against women are a threat to the church—rather than speaking of the necessity of their work. It is strange that it should imply that black Christians should stop their complaining about white privilege and racism in a society still so obviously imbalanced against minorities. It is strange that it should call activism for justice a *distraction* from the pure gospel while presenting the "biblical" view as passive and individualized—we "live justly" and "give others their due." It is strange that an evangelical statement on justice should be *so against it*.

## Biblical Justice

In contrast to this view of justice, the Bible is much stronger on justice as an active necessity for the church. Justice is all over the Bible. Consider the following examples.

### *The Ten Commandments and the Law of Love*

The Ten Commandments were the foundational principles of Israel's covenant. Books such as Exodus and Deuteronomy spend much of their duration explaining how these principles should operate in Israel's life. It is remarkable that so much of the application of "You shall not steal" in Deuteronomy is expressed in laws that insist that the rich should *provide for the poor* and cancel debts so that they might not be deprived of their inheritance for very long. In other words, failure to express generosity is the counterpart of theft. (This is in marked contrast to the modern gripe that social welfare programs steal from the employed to give to the lazy.)

In Luke 10, a lawyer approaches Jesus and asks "Teacher, what shall I do to inherit eternal life?" The exchange proceeds like this:

> "He said to him, 'What is written in the Law? How do you read it?' And he answered, 'You shall love the Lord your God with all

your heart and with all your soul and with all your strength and with all your mind, and your neighbor as yourself.' And he said to him, 'You have answered correctly; do this, and you will live.' But he, desiring to justify himself, said to Jesus, 'And who is my neighbor?'" (Luke 10:26–29)

The lawyer seems to have understood Jesus' command for him to do this as implying that he was not already doing so. In order to still be able to see himself as law-abiding, he begins fishing for Jesus to provide a definition of "neighbor" that leaves him on the right side of the law. Jesus responds with the parable of the Good Samaritan. According to this parable, love for one's neighbor means seeing even *an enemy* in desperate need and being willing to intervene on their behalf, even at great personal cost.

Doing justice does not mean *avoiding being the robber* or merely giving someone their due; it means action, restoration, and generosity to the other—even if they are not in your tribe or not deserving of your help.

### *The king as Executer of Justice*

Israel's kingship was intended to be an office in which the nation's leader executed justice and righteousness (see 2 Sam 8:15; 1 Kgs 10:9). Godly leadership was to lead the way in doing justice.

After the failure of Israel's monarchy, the prophets raised hopes in a divine Messiah who would fully and finally restore justice again.

> "Behold, the days are coming, declares the LORD, when I will raise up for David a righteous Branch, and he shall reign as king and deal wisely, and shall execute justice and righteousness in the land. In his days Judah will be saved, and Israel will dwell securely. And this is the name by which he will be called: 'The LORD is our righteousness.'" (Jer 23:5–6; see also Isa 16:5)

The mission of the Messiah, therefore, was to bring justice about for a nation subject to oppression. If our call is to imitate our Messiah, working for justice surely is also a key part of our mission as a church.

### *Injustice as the Motivation for Exile*

In 722 BC, the northern kingdom of Israel was taken into exile by the Assyrians who mixed the Israelite population with other conquered nations.

Between 597 and 586 BC, the Babylonians did similarly to the southern kingdom of Judah, taking them into captivity in Babylonia. Both these events were seen theologically as divine judgment—as the expulsion of God's people from his land. What is sometimes under-appreciated is that the prophets repeatedly identified *injustice* as a leading reason for the exiles. For example:

> "Thus says the LORD: 'For three transgressions of Israel, and for four, I will not revoke the punishment, because they sell the righteous for silver, and the needy for a pair of sandals—those who trample the head of the poor into the dust of the earth and turn aside the way of the afflicted; a man and his father go in to the same girl, so that my holy name is profaned; they lay themselves down beside every altar on garments taken in pledge, and in the house of their God they drink the wine of those who have been fined.'" (Amos 2:6–8)

> "'They do not know how to do right,' declares the LORD, 'those who store up violence and robbery in their strongholds.' Therefore thus says the Lord GOD: 'An adversary shall surround the land and bring down your defenses from you, and your strongholds shall be plundered.'" (Amos 3:10–11)[15]

We as New Covenant people do not live in a theocracy as Israel did. Our lands are not Promised Lands and our governments are not held to God's standards as Israel's were. In some ways, the demand to bring about justice in our lands is *less* acute than it was in the Old Testament.

However, the lesson should not be missed. God cares enough about injustice that he was willing to allow his land, his temple, and his Ark to be trampled and desecrated by vile and oppressive nations such as Babylon. If Israel would not be representatives of God's character, if they insisted on behaving as the other nations did, God was willing to shame himself and to let his nation be treated as other nations were.

Injustice was provocation enough that God reversed the great act of salvation of the Old Testament: the exodus. Instead of defeating the enemy power, they were crushed by it; instead of being brought into the land, they were cast out of it; instead of God constituting them as a nation, the nation was dismantled.

---

15. For more good examples, see also Isa 5:5–25; Mic 2:1–3; 3:1–12.

Justice and love for the outsider was a key characteristic of God's kingdom and a means by which Israel showed that God was among them. Its absence proved that they were just like the nations. We may not have the same Promised Land as they did in the Old Covenant, but we still have a God who cares about injustice just as much. We don't expect godly justice from our national leaders, but it is clearly an essential part of the character and witness of God's people that they represent his justice wherever they can.

*Jesus and Weightier Matters of the Law*

In the New Testament, the group that most often stands as the opponent of Jesus is the Pharisees. While we know them as the bad guys of Jewish religion of the first century, that is a characterization that would have been almost incomprehensible to most of their contemporaries. Even Jesus says: "For I tell you, unless your righteousness exceeds that of the scribes and Pharisees, you will never enter the kingdom of heaven," (Matt 5:20)—a self-defeating point unless the Pharisees were thought to be the *most righteous* of all.

Pharisees were the leading churchmen, the most law-abiding, the most concerned with holiness, and the most committed to their personal religion. Many of them in time became genuine followers of Jesus. When you think of a Pharisee, you should be thinking of the Christians that you know who are church leaders, lawful, holy, and committed. It is at those sorts of people that Jesus directs his harshest criticisms in all the Gospels.[16]

Jesus' condemnation of the Pharisees had to do with how deep their religion went. Although they kept themselves from breaking the law, and although they genuinely hoped to be the most faithful keepers of the covenant in all of Israel's history, they were so caught up with the details that they neglected to do the "weightier matters" of the law. On more than one occasion, Jesus says to them: "Go and learn what this means, 'I desire mercy, and not sacrifice,'" (e.g., Matt 9:13; 12:7).

In his long declarations of woe to the Pharisees, he says:

> "Woe to you, scribes and Pharisees, hypocrites! For you tithe mint and dill and cumin, and have neglected the weightier matters of

---

16. Of course the dear, holy, committed friend that you have in mind may not have the heart of a Pharisee, but the people who have the heart of a Pharisee do look like your friend!

the law: justice and mercy and faithfulness. These you ought to
have done, without neglecting the others." (Matt 23:23)

The thing that indicated that their religion was not genuine was that it did not produce hearts that cared enough about the injustice and suffering of others to get their hands dirty. They excelled at personal holiness, but for that their hands needed to be clean.

*James and True Religion*

Finally, returning to the book of James, the New Testament provides us with a picture of true religion:

> "But be doers of the word, and not hearers only, deceiving yourselves . . . But the one who looks into the perfect law, the law of liberty, and perseveres, being no hearer who forgets but a doer who acts, he will be blessed in his doing. If anyone thinks he is religious and does not bridle his tongue but deceives his heart, this person's religion is worthless. Religion that is pure and undefiled before God, the Father, is this: to visit orphans and widows in their affliction, and to keep oneself unstained from the world." (Jas 1:22, 26–27)

James identifies a few attributes that characterize those who truly possess and are possessed by the gospel:

- They are not those who hear the gospel—or even *celebrate* the gospel—but those who put it into practice.
- They are those who practice the "law of liberty"; while we tend to privatize such things (so that the gospel is about *my* liberty), it is likely that the more communally-minded thinking of the ancient world would see this as a characteristic of God's people. The law of liberty makes one "a doer who acts," most likely to secure liberty for those around them, both spiritually and bodily.
- An unbridled tongue—one that damages and deceives—is the antithesis of true religion.
- The definition of true religion is not only, like the Pharisee, to keep unpolluted by the world, but also to "visit orphans and widows in their distress."

The idea that the law of liberty means practicing justice is confirmed by this latter point: true religion means caring for the vulnerable. The sort of visitation in mind here is not merely a pastoral visit. In the Old Testament, giving justice and material provision for widows and orphans is an idiomatic picture of true justice, and oppression of widows and orphans as a picture of most extreme evil. For example:

> "You shall not pervert the justice due to the sojourner or to the fatherless, or take a widow's garment in pledge, but you shall remember that you were a slave in Egypt and the LORD your God redeemed you from there; therefore I command you to do this. When you reap your harvest in your field and forget a sheaf in the field, you shall not go back to get it. It shall be for the sojourner, the fatherless, and the widow, that the LORD your God may bless you in all the work of your hands." (Deut 24:17–19)

> "Sing to God, sing praises to his name; lift up a song to him who rides through the deserts; his name is the LORD; exult before him! Father of the fatherless and protector of widows is God in his holy habitation." (Ps 68:4)[17]

Widows and orphans were those without families who could look after their needs. They were the most vulnerable and the least able to repay their helpers. Caring for them was a mark of an altruist: someone who acted in sacrificial love and without the expectation of reward. Seeing as there is more of a safety-net for widows and orphans in our society and more opportunity for professional employment and self-sufficiency for adults, widows in particular might not be those in greatest need or most prone to exploitation any longer. The crucial thing is that we are required to care about those most in need, most in danger, and without any capacity to repay us. *That* is true religion, says James.

## Conclusion

Biblical hope is ultimately in the kingdom to arrive at the end of all things. It is this that should occupy our vision and shape the way that we live. It

---

17. See also some other examples in: Exod 22:22–24; Deut 10:17–19; 14:29; 16:11; 16:14; 26:12–13; 27:19; Job 22:9; 24:3; 24:21; Ps 94:6; 146:9; Isa 1:17, 23; Jer 7:6; 22:3; Ezek 22:7; Zech 7:10; Mal 3:5.

should cause us to prioritize a life that will bring real treasures into eternity—other people!

However, the Bible is clear that a heavenly-minded life and true Christian witness involves more than just waiting. We are to model kingdom living now. It is through seeing our life lived in imitation of God that people will glorify God on the day of his visitation.

Whether your definition of the gospel is narrow so that it excludes social justice or biblical-theological and inclusive of it, there is no question that godly living means the pursuit of justice and that this is at the very center of what it means to be a Christian. The old evangelical suspicion of social action is a hangover of the wars with liberal doctrine of the last century. But a Christian faith without social justice is a dead faith without hope. A Christian faith that images God's care for the unloved is one that paints eternal hope on the landscape of our world and gives our gospel preaching life.

> "I must confess that over the last few years I have been gravely disappointed with the white moderate. I have almost reached the regrettable conclusion that the Negro's great stumbling block in the stride toward freedom is not the White Citizens Councilor or the Ku Klux Klanner but the white moderate who is more devoted to order than to justice; who prefers a negative peace which is the absence of tension to a positive peace which is the presence of justice; who constantly says, 'I agree with you in the goal you seek, but I can't agree with your methods of direct action'; who paternalistically feels that he can set the timetable for another man's freedom; who lives by the myth of time; and who constantly advises the Negro to wait until a 'more convenient season.' Shallow understanding from people of good will is more frustrating than absolute misunderstanding from people of ill will. Lukewarm acceptance is much more bewildering than outright rejection . . . I had the strange feeling when I was suddenly catapulted into the leadership of the bus protest in Montgomery several years ago that we would have the support of the white church. I felt that the white ministers, priests, and rabbis of the South would be some of our strongest allies. Instead, some few have been outright opponents, refusing to understand the freedom movement and misrepresenting its leaders; all too many others have been more cautious than courageous and have remained silent behind the anesthetizing security of stained-glass windows . . . In the midst of a mighty struggle to rid our nation of racial and economic injustice, I have heard

so many ministers say, 'Those are social issues which the gospel has nothing to do with,' and I have watched so many churches commit themselves to a completely otherworldly religion which made a strange distinction between bodies and souls, the sacred and the secular."[18]

---

18. King, *Letter from Birmingham Jail*.

## Chapter 10

# Love

*Now concerning food offered to idols: we know that "all of us possess knowledge." This "knowledge" puffs up, but love builds up. If anyone imagines that he knows something, he does not yet know as he ought to know. But if anyone loves God, he is known by God. (1 Cor 8:1–3)*

"Doctrine divides, love unites!"

This is an old rallying cry of the ecumenical movement, which aimed to promote common ground upon which all Christians could unite. A major obstacle to finding common ground is doctrine—after all, our denominations tend to be gathered around theological differences—and so the approach to unity was to rid Christians of our focus on doctrine, and rather to emphasize the biblical command to love as an ethical principle that could transcend old divisions.

Evangelical churches have been strongly resistant to this slogan, because it threatens to cut the church loose from thousands of years of theological struggle and careful study of truth and error in interpretation, and to replace it with an anything-goes attitude towards theology. As the Scriptures warn us, we can't have unity with those who scandalize the body of Christ by lives of open sin or with those whose teaching is in opposition to the apostolic gospel. Truth matters, and love based on disregard for truth is a warped, weak-middled kind of love. If those who die outside of Christ will be subject to God's judgement, then such "love" for people denies them truth and denies them hope. It is *unloving* to see someone on the wrong path and to do nothing for fear of division.

We surely should agree that the gospel is the heart of Christian teaching, and that without gospel doctrine souls will be lost. Doctrineless unity might make it easier to love one another, but it is a unity that is most likely won *at the cost of* the gospel, not inspired by it.

However, we ought also to agree that the Bible is opposed to division, and demands from us—perhaps more than anything else—that we love another. Doctrine *does* divide, and love *does* unite. The ecumenical *solution* is a wrong turn, but their slogan does capture some of the truth.

## God is Love

Among the attributes that God declares as essential to his Trinitarian being are mercy and grace (Exod 34:6), holiness (Lev 11:45), and love. Love is the core ethic of the Christian religion:

> "Beloved, let us love one another, for love is from God, and whoever loves has been born of God and knows God. Anyone who does not love does not know God, *because God is love*. In this the love of God was made manifest among us, that God sent his only Son into the world, so that we might live through him. In this is love, not that we have loved God but that he loved us and *sent his Son* to be the propitiation for our sins. *Beloved, if God so loved us, we also ought to love one another*. No one has ever seen God; if we love one another, God abides in us and his love is perfected in us. By this we know that we abide in him and he in us, because he has *given us of his Spirit* . . . So we have come to know and to believe the love that God has for us. *God is love*, and whoever abides in love abides in God, and God abides in him . . . We love because he first loved us. If anyone says, 'I love God,' and hates his brother, he is a liar; for he who does not love his brother whom he has seen cannot love God whom he has not seen. And this commandment we have from him: *whoever loves God must also love his brother*."
> (1 John 4:7–13, 16, 19–21)

While love is natural to God, it is alien to us. Selfishness is our natural state. It is possible to practice theology while ruled by selfishness. It is possible to practice church discipline while ruled by selfishness. It is possible to enter relationships in order to practice *self*-love. But it is not possible to love truly while ruled by selfishness.

Love is not as much an attribute of the emotions as it is an attribute of the will. We *can* feel love, but even if we don't, we must still *choose* it. Love is the commitment to seek the good of others. It is the opposite of selfishness and its counterpart: hate. For this reason, while love is modelled for us in Christ with crystal clarity—love is self-sacrificial service even of the undeserving—it is still repeated and explained and commanded in the Scriptures because we are so bad at it.

## Love and Freedom

As 1 John 4 points out, we cannot claim to love God while also hating those around us.

In the months after the "Arab Spring" movement that took place in the Middle East, there was a spate of Islamic terrorist reprisals in Egypt, particularly against Coptic Christians, leading to dozens of deaths. At the height of terrorist threat, a group of Muslims banded together in opposition to what they viewed as an assault on Egypt itself. They surrounded the Virgin Mary Church in Cairo during the Christmas Eve Mass celebration—the sort of event that ISIS terrorists had been targeting—and volunteered themselves as *human shields*.

> "Among those shields were movie stars Adel Imam and Yousra, popular Muslim televangelist and preacher Amr Khaled, the two sons of President Hosni Mubarak, and thousands of citizens."[1]

It was a remarkable show of solidarity and love for outsiders that members of an opposing religion would put their own lives in harm's way in order to serve Christian worshippers.

While there will be examples of such behavior from Christian communities too, *all of us* who bear that name should be front-runners in love for the unloved. Unfortunately, this is very often not the case. There was strong conservative support, even from evangelicals, for the recent travel bans on Muslims—preventing even American Muslims who had traveled before the ban from returning to their families—simply because of fear and racial distrust. Or, to return to an easy target, the members of Westboro Baptist regard it as a *ministry* to proclaim God's "hatred" of homosexual

---

1. El-Rashidi, *Egypt's Muslims Attend Coptic Christmas Mass*.

outsiders and they have even run a counter on their website logging how many days a certain gay son has been burning in hell since his death. Perhaps they are the most extreme in their expression of baptized hatred, but diluted expressions of the same attitude are far too common.

Our zeal for truth and holiness often is misdirected, and we forget that Jesus commanded us to love our enemies—to bless and not to curse. We ignore a tragically under-appreciated instruction from Paul to keep our judgement in-house and to leave outsiders alone, preferring instead to condemn outsiders and leave double-minded church members in peace:

> "I wrote to you in my letter not to associate with sexually immoral people—not at all meaning the sexually immoral of this world, or the greedy and swindlers, or idolaters, since then you would need to go out of the world ... For what have I to do with judging outsiders? Is it not those inside the church whom you are to judge? God judges those outside. "Purge the evil person from among you." (1 Cor 5:9–10, 12–13)

First Corinthians 5 doesn't imply that we should *approve* of sinful behavior in the world, and we are free as citizens to argue for laws that we regard as best for society, but we don't stand as *judges* of the nations in which we live as exiles. Paul doesn't seem to want us to throw condemnations at the LGBTQIA+ community, for example; he wants us to *associate* with them. If we are to love them, it means that we are to seek their good even to our own hurt. For all of us as evangelicals, that means bringing them to Christ, but how can we do that if our attitude is one of disgust or hostility? How many of this community would you guess Westboro Baptist has led to Christ? We need to be able to lead people out of moral and spiritual lostness, but how will we ever have the room to talk about change if we lose the ability to talk to such people altogether?

Evangelicals are often quick to talk about the obligations of moral law and quick to condemn those who fall short. It is very *easy* to persuade a non-Christian that they are law-breakers—particularly if God himself is the moral standard to which we hold them. From there, the evangelist simply has to tell their target that God through Christ can deal with those sins. It is wonderful that God has used this approach to save many. But is that really our gospel?

To the Pharisees and scribes—those most consumed with God's law—Jesus said:

> "But woe to you, scribes and Pharisees, hypocrites! For you shut the kingdom of heaven in people's faces. For you neither enter yourselves nor allow those who would enter to go in. Woe to you, scribes and Pharisees, hypocrites! For you travel across sea and land to make a single proselyte, and when he becomes a proselyte, you make him twice as much a child of hell as yourselves." (Matt 23:13, 15)
>
> "And he said, 'Woe to you lawyers also! For you load people with burdens hard to bear, and you yourselves do not touch the burdens with one of your fingers.'" (Luke 11:46)

Jesus targeted the religious elite of his day, not because God's law wasn't important, but because the *focus* on God's law distracted from what the law was supposed to be about—relationships with God and others restored. If we overemphasize law in our gospel preaching, we run the risk of implying that the Christian life is about compliance, which in turn places a burden on believers that cuts against the actual gospel.

In response to burdensome religion, Jesus made a counter-offer:

> "Come to me, all who labor and are heavy laden, and I will give you rest. Take my yoke upon you, and learn from me, for I am gentle and lowly in heart, and you will find rest for your souls. For my yoke is easy, and my burden is light." (Matt 11:28–30)

There are some interesting tensions in this text. Jesus makes the invitation to those who labor and carry heavy burdens. He invites them to come to him to enjoy rest. Curiously, this rest involves putting on a *yoke*. It is apparently not the absence of labor, but a new kind of labor—one that is easy; a burden that is light. Furthermore, it appears to be labor that has already been modeled by Christ himself—we are to learn from his example. And what is that example? He is gentle and lowly in heart. By learning from him and laboring as he did, we find rest for our souls.

It seems as though Jesus is calling to those who labor (whatever that might be—whether religious exertions, efforts to please God, efforts to free ourselves from guilt) and whose labor lays a restless heaviness upon their souls. He doesn't invite us to *leisure*—we are now to labor at following Jesus' example of gentleness and humility—but this labor means release of our souls from burden.

In Galatians, Paul is writing against the influence of Judaizers who believed that Gentiles could not be followers of Jesus without first becoming

Jews.[2] Paul taught that the New Covenant upheld the law in a new way and that the Old Covenant was no longer necessary. God had already demonstrated his acceptance of the Gentiles apart from the Law by giving them the Spirit. Those who wanted Gentile converts first to take on the yoke of the Torah were adding restrictions that God had not demanded of them. In response, Galatians is full of the idea of gospel freedom:

> "Yet because of false brothers secretly brought in—who slipped in to spy out our freedom that we have in Christ Jesus, so that they might bring us into slavery—to them we did not yield in submission even for a moment, so that the truth of the gospel might be preserved for you." (Gal 2:4–5)

> "For freedom Christ has set us free; stand firm therefore, and do not submit again to a yoke of slavery . . . For you were called to freedom, brothers. Only do not use your freedom as an opportunity for the flesh, but through love serve one another. For the whole law is fulfilled in one word: 'You shall love your neighbor as yourself.' But if you bite and devour one another, watch out that you are not consumed by one another." (Gal 5:1, 13–15)

In these texts, Paul is strongly against anything that imposes a burden upon people that the gospel does not compel us to bear. The law is good—he himself says as much (1 Tim 1:8; Rom 7:12), and he even had Timothy circumcised because it made no difference except to open up ministry possibilities (Acts 16:3)—but the old religious observances are not the *gospel*. It is for freedom that Christ set us free, and our law is that of love. We are not slaves again to the law, and our Spirit is not one of fear (Rom 8:15).

Paul adds an important qualification: "Only do not use your freedom as an opportunity for the flesh"—we do have obligations to the law of love and service of others, not to indulge selfishness. Jesus does place on us a new yoke. Nevertheless, the gospel must be understood in the right order. We do not impose rules that, if followed, allow *some room* for freedom. We preach a gospel of liberty, and within that liberty lies our law: we are freed to love God and one another. Our gospel teaching should not in any way be able to be confused (as it so often is) with a system of rules, or even a system of good-but-secondary theological issues that we've promoted to a

---

2. Christianity and Judaism were not popularly regarded as different faiths at that time.

status that they don't possess.[3] The imposition of small human slaveries to our gospel breeds a spirit that provokes us to bite and devour one another.

Our gospel means that we are freed to love. That is our law.

## Love and Unity

> "Once I saw this guy on a bridge about to jump. I said, 'Don't do it!' He said, 'Nobody loves me.' I said, 'God loves you. Do you believe in God?'
>
> He said, 'Yes.' I said, 'Are you a Christian or a Jew?' He said, 'A Christian.' I said, 'Me, too! Protestant or Catholic?' He said, 'Protestant.' I said, 'Me, too! What franchise?' He said, 'Baptist.' I said, 'Me, too! Northern Baptist or Southern Baptist?' He said, 'Northern Baptist.' I said, 'Me, too! Northern Conservative Baptist or Northern Liberal Baptist?'
>
> He said, 'Northern Conservative Baptist.' I said, 'Me, too! Northern Conservative Baptist Great Lakes Region, or Northern Conservative Baptist Eastern Region?' He said, 'Northern Conservative Baptist Great Lakes Region.' I said, 'Me, too! Northern Conservative Baptist Great Lakes Region Council of 1879, or Northern Conservative Baptist Great Lakes Region Council of 1912?' He said, 'Northern Conservative Baptist Great Lakes Region Council of 1912.' I said, 'Die, heretic!' And I pushed him over."[4]

"Doctrine divides; love unites."

While studying Phil 2:1–11 recently, I was prompted to think of this slogan again. As with the man in Emo Philips's joke, if we define ourselves first by our doctrinal particularities, variation in doctrine will necessarily create an in-group and an out-group—those who subscribe to our theological definition and those who don't. Of course theology is important—the Bible warns repeatedly about false teachers who threaten to kidnap us from

---

3. Rom 6:15 suggests that Paul's teaching of grace was taken to imply that there were no rules and that people could sin with impunity. Paul denies this, but it is notable that his gospel gave Christians *more freedom* than his contemporaries were comfortable with. It is true that he goes on in this chapter to compare our gospel to a move from slavery under one master (sin) to another (Christ), but he acknowledges that this is a human and imperfect analogy ("I am speaking in human terms, because of your natural limitations," 6:19). He goes on to emphasize freedom again: we are set free (6:22) and we receive a free gift of eternal life (6:23). In chapter 7 he abandons the slavery metaphor altogether and adopts the picture of a marriage relationship instead.

4. Philips, *Best God Joke Ever*.

our hope—but the Bible repeatedly encourages unity and peace too. If our identity as believers is based on our own theological preferences, we are likely to keep dividing from those who challenge our identity. This passage in Philippians, however, seems to me to model doctrine and love in the right order and in the right balance:

> "So if there is any encouragement in Christ, any comfort from love, any participation in the Spirit, any affection and sympathy, complete my joy by being of the same mind, having the same love, being in full accord and of one mind. Do nothing from selfish ambition or conceit, but in humility count others more significant than yourselves. Let each of you look not only to his own interests, but also to the interests of others." (Phil 2:1–4)

The motivation for unity in this passage is absolutely not the *rejection* of doctrine—it is firmly based on the gospel core. However, the order in which it presents its appeal for unity is not by ruling on whose theology in the conflict in Philippi is correct, but by first establishing the *ethic upon which unity is possible*. If our gospel means that we have experienced love and encouragement in Christ, affection, mercy, and the participation in the Spirit that Christians all share, then this ought to issue in the same kind of love and agreement in mind with others that we have experienced in God. Given what God has overlooked in us and what errors in our thinking he has tolerated in order to unite us with himself, we also ought to express the same grace to others. Paul urges us to be "co-souled" with one another and to share one mind. He urges us to express humility and concern for the interests of the other, rather than defending our own names and preferences.

The great hymn of Christ that follows (2:5–11)—a stunning example of a common theological foundation—emphasizes the humility and self-sacrifice of Christ, who descended into shame and suffered for our redemption, and who waited for God to vindicate and glorify him, though he could have demanded the glory due to him if he had wanted to. This is given as the model for us to follow in our own interpersonal relationships, particularly when in conflict.

In other words, the work and example of Christ and the unity of the Spirit sets a model for our treatment of one another, and this ethos is able to produce unity with others in the wider church family. Loving one another (our ethic) and having the same mind (our gospel unity) are put in balance. Humility and love are the ground upon which unity and diversity can co-exist.

So, while it is a foolish reaction to theological infighting to discard doctrine, there is substantial emphasis in this passage—and throughout the Bible—on love as the core Christian ethic. Theology represents our best efforts to understand our faith and it is important to that degree, but it is the gospel message and the ethic of love that should be at the core. If we agree on the gospel and if we are committed to working for the interests of others, our theological differences need not divide us.

## Disunity in Diversity

There are many examples from church history of theological debates that were perhaps important, but which led to huge fissures in the Christian church.

Long before the Reformation divided the Catholic (i.e., "universal") Church in Western Europe,[5] the universal church underwent what was perhaps an even bigger division, splitting into Roman Catholicism and Eastern Orthodoxy. One major factor (though not the only) in the split was a difference of opinion on the addition by the Western church of the so-called "Filioque Clause" into the Nicene Creed: the question was whether or not the Holy Spirit proceeds from the Father alone, or from the Father *and* the son ("filioque"). The Western churches preferred to have the clause included in the creed, because for them it underlined that Father and Son were of one substance.[6] The East wanted it excluded, because they believed that it diminished the importance of the Holy Spirit and led to doctrinal errors. Eventually, in 1054, after further accusations of heresy, the Christian world split in two—as it is to this day.

While the doctrine of the Trinity is very important, because it concerns what God is like and it is the basis for Jesus' atoning sacrifice and the core ethic of love, the being of God is a mystery that is beyond us and not fully revealed in Scripture. Furthermore, while I am sure taking or leaving the Filioque Clause and then running hard in your chosen direction might have the potential to lead to error, has anyone—*anyone*—found that this controversy has impacted their discipleship one way or another? I for one have never heard teaching on the subject outside of the academy, I can think of very few Scriptures that are relevant to it, I doubt that the vast majority of evangelical Christians have ever heard of the dispute or the

---

5. A justifiable division, in this case, given that it concerned gospel essentials.
6. Gonzalez, *Story of Christianity*, 264–5.

doctrine, and I can't think of a single problem of Christian living that can be clearly linked to this clause.

It is also odd that on a theological issue, the world could be so neatly divided into hemispheres—i.e., why did the whole of the West think one way and the whole of the East another? Brains don't all follow the same pattern unless they've been primed to think so or explicitly pressured to think so. Tribal thinking ought not to be possible if we hold to the gospel core and its ethic of love. I can see no reason why a church consumed with love for the other and humility about one's own knowledge should have divided over this matter.

The Protestant Reformation had its own problems with division, especially concerning baptism, and disputes led to violence and persecution of one group against the other. Almost five-hundred years later, we continue to have denominations organized along baptismal lines, and mutual misunderstanding and suspicion still persists.

Most evangelicals see repeated appeals in Scripture for unity, but we also take our divisions for granted. Our approach to unity is to attempt to secure conformity to the theological positions that our specific community prefers—we try to unify as widely as possible upon a *homogenous* theological foundation.

However, unity within narrow traditions is not unity. It is a partial consensus that we've given a name. This is the only unity that hard adherence to secondary issues is able to produce. By contrast, if we unify on the gospel core and reduce the number of secondary issues that keep us apart, there is far more scope for sharing the same mind. If we are to express both unity and truth in our churches, we need to hold tightly to the white-hot gospel center of our faith and loosely and humbly to everything else.

## Unity in Diversity

If our theological differences are removed from their position at the center of how we define ourselves then we have greater freedom to express diversity without division.

Vanhoozer, writing about biblical truth, says something that is appropriate to us as God's people too:

> "Truth, like reality, is in one sense one. However, reality is so rich and multifaceted that it, like white light, can only be conveyed verbally by an equally rich spectrum—diverse literary forms . . . That

> Scripture has many literary forms is no impediment to the truth. Instead, it is the very possibility of truth's expression. The diversity of literary forms does not imply that Scripture contains competing kinds of truth . . . Revealed truth may be said in many ways."[7]

God has revealed truth to us in many literary forms because truth is a multifaceted thing; there is depth and complexity to all of life that defies neat capture by one mode of thought or expression. In a similar way, theological diversity among Christians is not a challenge to be *overcome* (except concerning matters of the gospel core), but an opportunity for us to perceive greater depth in our appreciation of the Christian life and to learn from one another. You need me to correct and deepen how you think and read the Bible, and I need you.

If, as Philippians teaches us, we live under an ethic of love, gentleness, humility, and commitment to the needs of others—if *this* is the core of our identity—then theological diversity will be an opportunity for learning and growth, not a catalyst for division.

## Love and Evangelism

At the center of God's being is love. As one God in three persons, he expresses other-person-centered relationship within himself. *Restoring* relationship is the heart of God's mission in the world—the mission to which he has also called us. Unity is not a nice-to-have; it is evidence that the gospel is real.

In Deuteronomy, Moses speaks about the laws and rules of the Old Covenant, not as the means by which Israel attained salvation, but as central to their testimony to the nations of God's greatness:

> "See, I have taught you statutes and rules, as the LORD my God commanded me, that you should do them in the land that you are entering to take possession of it. Keep them and do them, for that will be your wisdom and your understanding in the sight of the peoples, who, when they hear all these statutes, will say, 'Surely this great nation is a wise and understanding people.' For what great nation is there that has a god so near to it as the LORD our God is to us, whenever we call upon him? And what great nation is there, that has statutes and rules so righteous as all this law that I set before you today?" (Deut 4:5–8)

---

7. Vanhoozer quoted in Long, *Art of Biblical History*, 91–92.

The nations looking in at Israel were meant to observe the justice of God's laws, the wisdom of the people, and the nearness of their God. The law, summarized as it was by the principle of love, would demonstrate the righteousness of God and his people.

In the same way, in the New Testament, Jesus tells us that our love for one another is a crucial part of our witness to the world. "By this all people will know that you are my disciples, if you have love for one another" (John 13:35). In John 17:20–23, Jesus says a similar thing about unity. Jesus prays that we would be *perfectly one* so that "the world may know that you sent me and loved them even as you loved me." Consider the gravity of these verses. If people see us living changed lives of love, it makes our message that our God is love much more potent. If people see us living lives of self-righteousness and hypocrisy, our gospel message rings hollow. If people see our unity, they will know that Jesus is real and really at work. If we are divided and divisive, it makes a mockery of the claim that we are united with Christ.

Can any of the culture wars that we engage in that apparently have such high stakes match the importance of our unity or lack thereof? Would Jesus say that by our creationism people will know that God sent him and loves us? And yet we're more likely to preach that it's a problem to be united with evolutionists than we are to preach that it's a problem to be disunited.

## Conclusion

We are called to imitate God—the God who *is* love. This means replacing our innate selfishness with a heart of love for others. Unity is not possible if we elevate secondary issues to levels of gospel importance and insist on our own theological rightness. This smacks of selfishness rather than love.

If, on the other hand, we directed the same level of zeal at cultivating the imitation of God's *character*—humility and gentleness and love—we would have a genuine chance at gospel unity, at learning from each other's strengths, and presenting the watching world with a compelling vision of a transformed community. In this way, even though they accuse us of evil, onlookers would "see your good deeds and glorify God on the day of visitation" (1 Pet 2:12).

> "Finally, brothers and sisters, rejoice. Aim for restoration, comfort one another, agree with one another, live in peace; and the God of love and peace will be with you." (2 Cor 13:11)

CHAPTER 11

# Centered Evangelicalism

*And above all these put on love, which binds everything together in perfect harmony. And let the peace of Christ rule in your hearts, to which indeed you were called in one body. And be thankful. (Col 3:14–15)*

HIROO ONODA WAS AN intelligence officer who fought for Japan in the Second World War and is arguably their most famous soldier from that conflict. The Japanese held to a doctrine of honor that meant a soldier would rather die than shame himself by surrendering. This commitment had obvious benefits, ensuring that soldiers prized the needs of the army above even their own lives and that they would never give up. This made it all the more surprising when the Japanese nation surrendered in 1945. It was so surprising that Onoda didn't believe it.

Onoda was part of a unit stationed in the Philippines and tasked with engaging in guerrilla warfare. They were cut off from civilization and out of contact with Japanese command. When leaflets were dropped in 1945 in an attempt to notify the soldiers in the mountains that the war was over, Onoda found the communication to be too error-strewn to be genuinely Japanese and he took it to be enemy propaganda. Eventually, almost thirty years after the end of the war, Onoda was located and his aged commanding officer, now a bookseller, had to be brought in to decommission him before he would surrender. Onoda had lost an additional twenty-nine years of his life and killed thirty people in that time in the exercise of his "duty."[1]

The idea of a quixotic soldier waging war against an imaginary foe for decades, taking lives and losing so much of his own, is both amusing and tragic. It's foolish to have a business-as-usual attitude when one's nation is at war, but it is also destructive to have a wartime attitude in days of peace. Onoda treated those who were trying to give him good news as enemies. He killed *thirty* Philippine citizens for the glory of long-surrendered Japan.

## War and Peace

The more that the political and religious worlds have polarized, the more necessary it has become to use wartime language in service of the goals of one's own faction. As with the one-man World War of Hiroo Onoda, there is a tragic human cost to using these tactics in peacetime. There are many reasons why leaders might buy into using this sort of language. They might do it because the language of fear and threat more easily gets attention than the language of peace and love. They might do so because their job after the next voting cycle depends on motivating the electorate. They might do it because their opponent's polarizing language has made the opposition intimidating enough to require a response of equal strength.

Whatever the reason, the language of war puts life-or-death stakes on the conflicts that we engage in, and it pressures us to use win-at-all costs tactics in service of our own ends. What do you do if you have to choose to vote either for a corrupt candidate that is a betrayal of your own values or for the *enemy*? You're not a traitor are you? Where will your values be when the enemy is in charge and your whole way of life has been lost? Surely a little compromise now is for the greater good?

The increasing polarization of the modern political landscape into right and left has dragged evangelicalism into the muck with it. The language of war has exerted pressure on the church to identify conservative Christianity with conservative politics and the bouquet of ideological commitments that come with it, regardless of the compromises involved in that partnership.

Wartime language greatly reduces the tolerance that people have for complications and grey areas. "Life or death" is as black-and-white as it gets. If lives—*eternal* lives, no less—are at stake, there is little room for doubts

---

1. Davis, *Soldier Refused to Surrender*.

and open questions. The vocal segment of the church that is most convinced that we're at war is thus also the segment that places the most value on *certainty*—in our theologies, in our traditions, and in our ethos. In spite of the fact that Scripture repeatedly urges humility and criticizes human pride, Christians seem more often to be in denial of our own limitations as interpreters, and overconfident in our own abilities and our own rightness.

A knock-on effect of prizing certainty is that *challenges* to that certainty are experienced as threat. Someone who differs from us in areas that we consider important to our theological identity provides a source of intolerable uncertainty and danger to our identity. As such, the insiders must be pressured to keep faith in the group's certainties, but the outsider must be treated with hostility in order to repel their bad influence.

Certainty and rigidity appeal to some people, and so evangelicalism of this type will always find adherents full of encouragement of such behavior. However, living outside of a truly Christ-like ethos harms our evangelism and makes hypocrites of us. It cuts against our calling to love, and faith, and humility. Outsiders will see our errors and evident foolishness even if we won't.

## Waging the Good Warfare

You may well protest that it is not an errant wing of the church that declares us at war; *the Bible* does that. And it is foolish to risk the complacency of peacetime when engaged in a battle. Of course, this is true.

However, this is warfare of a particular kind, and it demands a kind of fighting that bears no resemblance to the kind of fighting that we've been discussing so far. This is what Paul tells Timothy:

> "This charge I entrust to you, Timothy, my child, in accordance with the prophecies previously made about you, that by them you may *wage the good warfare, holding faith and a good conscience*. By rejecting this, some have made shipwreck of their faith." (1 Tim 1:18–19)

There is a good warfare that we engage in, and according to Paul here, it is a war of perseverance—both in faith and conduct. The "good fight" that he encourages Timothy to fight in 1 Tim 6:11–12 involves the pursuit of "righteousness, godliness, faith, love, steadfastness, gentleness." The famous passage concerning the armor of God encourages God's people to fight with truth, peace, faith, and prayer, so that "you may be able to withstand in the evil day, and having done all, to stand firm" (Eph 6:10–18).

The war that Christians fight is, paradoxically, a war of love and peace. We fight spiritual warfare, and yet the fruit of the Spirit are all humble, other-centered qualities that we praise much and practice little:

> "But the fruit of the Spirit is love, joy, peace, patience, kindness, goodness, faithfulness, gentleness, self-control; against such things there is no law." (Gal 5:22–23)

In other words, if war produces unflinching commitment to the cause, it is important to recognize that the war that we're meant to be fighting is one of *good character and Christian perseverance*. At all costs we pursue a no-compromise attitude to love even our enemies, and to do those things that guard our discipleship of Christ. While we tend to want to be right and to divide from those who differ from us, the New Testament is consistent in imploring us to be the kind of people who are humble, who listen to reason, who are kind, and eager to serve (e.g., Jas 3:17–18). It is consistent in calling us to peace and unity (e.g., 1 Pet 3:8–11).[2]

Engaging in this warfare of peace and love has the ability to change our enemies to disciples. Look at what Peter says:

> "Beloved, I urge you as sojourners and exiles to abstain from the passions of the flesh, which wage war against your soul. Keep your conduct among the Gentiles honorable, so that when they speak against you as evildoers, they may see your good deeds and glorify God on the day of visitation." (1 Pet 2:11–12)

As exiles in this world, Peter says, Christians ought to wage war not on our host nations, but on *our own passions*. By keeping our way of life pure, any accusations that our opponents might bring against us would be refuted by our good conduct. While it is not clear here that these enemies are glorifying God willingly, in 1 Pet 3:1, he says that our honorable behavior is a tool by which we win opponents over. But if our behavior is dishonorable, there's no doubt that we're losing the war.

The cold fact is that if the whole world rejected evolution, they would most likely be looking for the next scientific explanation and be no closer to Christ. If the whole Western world rejected feminism, it would be no more

---

2. Division is a last resort, reserved for those who sin flagrantly and without repentance (Matt 18; 1 Cor 5), or those whose teaching endangers the gospel. Yet, even false teachers are to be corrected with gentleness and patience (2 Tim 2:23–26).

Christian than the patriarchal societies that feminism has not reached. If the whole church became premillennialist, it would not guarantee our unity in any other respect, we would not know Jesus better or love him more, and not a single soul would have joined us in our walk. If we managed to pressure the outside world into giving us our way on gay marriage, abortion, and so on, we might be happier with the morality of our laws, but it will have done little to restrain the morality of people[3] and nothing to introduce them to Christ. On the contrary, if we insist on fighting with the weapons that we have been using, rather than the humble, self-sacrificial attitude of love and service that the Spirit gives us to use, we might have done more to put them off of the gospel than to commend it to them.

The polarized culture war that evangelicals have chosen to fight is a dirty, bloodied campaign to prevent the world from encroaching on us. Yet Christ has commissioned us to *change the world*—he has commissioned us to make disciples and to wash one another's feet. It is this and this alone that has the power to succeed.

The ability of evangelicals to have a clear witness in our current society is being eroded at an alarming rate by arrogant certainty in our own rightness and compromise in our ethos. Rather than joining secular society in polarizing into hostile camps on the right and the left, evangelicals need to re-center and regain our gospel identity.

## The Return to Centered Evangelicalism

The centered evangelical ethos is based on the following principles:

1. We believe in Christ, the Word of God, and the centrality of his life, death, and resurrection to everything that we do. His death is the means by which we begin the gospel life, and he is the model on which we live out the gospel in the present. The gospel of God-with-us, restoring us to himself, is the core of our faith in which we put our trust and on which we base our unity.

2. We believe that Scripture is the word of God and the primary source of revelation of God and his gospel. God's inspiration of Scripture means that it is true and the final authority over our faith and practice.

---

3. See Col 2:20–23.

3. The interpretation of Scripture requires us to practice the hermeneutic of suspicion—that is, radical doubt in ourselves as interpreters. We adopt an interpretive ethos of humility, because we acknowledge that in our natural state we serve our own interests not the interests of others. We are subject to limitations of ability and the ongoing corrupting effects of sin. As a result, we must remain open to correction and growth in knowledge from any source by which God chooses to bring it. We pursue an interpretive community of social and theological diversity—founded on the gospel core—as an acknowledgement that we are often blind to our own weakness and error.

4. We conduct our discipleship in a posture of openness, not fear. We remain firm in our commitment to the gospel core, and we allow freedom and free discussion with regard to unclear and secondary issues. Who are you to pass judgment on the servant of another? It is before our own master that we stand or fall (Rom 14:4).

5. We pursue the law of love for enemies taught to us and modeled by Christ. This extends to our relationships, in which we practice self-sacrifice for the good of others, and our thinking, in which we practice gentleness and respect, and love for deep truth. Our ethos reflects the gifts and fruit of the Spirit.

6. Our hope is in the coming return of Christ to consummate his kingdom in the new heavens and new earth. As a demonstration of that hope and as imitation of God's character, it is a Christian imperative to pursue peace and justice and to invite others to join us in our hope—evangelism and social justice are connected and a primary part of Christian living. The *message* of the gospel only becomes good news when it is lived out; the gospel doesn't exist as a dead letter or a concept that resides in the realm of ideas. One can't pursue the gospel without justice. The two belong together. Faith without works is dead.

Evangelical faith might be more than this, but it is not less. If we genuinely possess a high view of Scripture and if it genuinely is our first and final authority, then we ought to obey it. This means pursuing the Great Commission above the needs of Christendom; this means guarding the truth of the gospel above our personal convictions; this means pursuing love and unity above our comfort and our preferences.

Christ must be our center or our faith and our calling are hollow.

# Bibliography

Alter, Robert. *The Five Books of Moses*. New York: WW Norton & Company, 2004.
Barton, John. *The Nature of Biblical Criticism*. Louisville, KY: Westminster John Knox, 2007.
Bell, Philip. "Proclaiming Creation in a Scientific Age." *Creation Ministries International Update: For Partners of CMI* (May 2015) 1–3. https://longwind.files.wordpress.com/2015/06/proclaiming_creation.pdf.
Borg, Marcus J. *Convictions: How I Learned What Matters Most*. New York: HarperCollins, 2014.
Bridge, Donald, and David Phypers. *The Waters That Divide*. Ross-shire: Mentor, 1998.
Buettel, Cameron. *Evangelical Syncretism: Submitting to Feminism*. 2015. https://www.gty.org/library/blog/B150219/evangelical-syncretism-submitting-to-feminism.
Butler, Rex D. *History of Christianity 2: Anabaptists*. 2007. https://www.nobts.edu/faculty/atoh/ButlerR-files/CH2_Unit_1e.Anabaptists.ppt.
Chalmers, Aaron. The Influence of Cognitive Biases on Biblical Interpretation. *Bulletin for Biblical Research* 26, no. 4 (2016) 467–80.
Davis, Matt. *Why a Japanese WWII Soldier Refused to Surrender for 29 Years*. 2019. https://bigthink.com/politics-current-affairs/wwii-soldier-refused-surrender-29-years.
Dawkins, Richard. *The God Delusion*. New York: Houghton Mifflin, 2006.
Defending Inerrancy. *What is Biblical Inerrancy?* 2014. http://defendinginerrancy.com/why-is-inerrancy-important.
Dunning, David. "The Dunning–Kruger Effect: On Being Ignorant of One's Own Ignorance." In *Advances in Experimental Social Psychology, Volume 44*, edited by Mark P. Zanna and James M. Olsen, 247–96. Cambridge, MA: Academic Press, 2011.
Egginton, William. *What is Fundamentalism?* 2011. https://arcade.stanford.edu/blogs/what-fundamentalism.
El-Rashidi, Yasmine. *Egypt's Muslims Attend Coptic Christmas Mass, Serving as "Human Shields."* 2011. http://english.ahram.org.eg/News/3365.aspx.
Eskenazi, Tamara Cohn. "Torah as Narrative and Narrative as Torah." In *Old Testament Interpretation: Past, Present, and Future: Essays in Honor of Gene M. Tucker*, edited by James Luther Mays, David L. Petersen and Kent Harold Richards, 13–30. Nashville, TN: Abingdon Press, 1995.
France, R T. *Women in the Church's Ministry: A Test-case for Biblical Hermeneutics*. Carlisle: Paternoster, 1995.
Geisler, Norman L. *J. I. Packer Stands Firm on Inerrancy*. 2017. http://defendinginerrancy.com/j-i-packer-stands-firm-on-inerrancy/.

# Bibliography

———. *Methodological Unorthodoxy*. 2003. http://normangeisler.com/methodological-unorthodoxy/.

———. *The ETS Vote on Robert Gundry at their Annual Meeting in December*. 1983. https://normangeisler.com/the-ets-vote-on-robert-gundry-at-their-annual-meeting-in-december-1983/.

Geisler, Norman L, and Thomas Howe. *1 Samuel 1:1—Was Elkanah, the Father of Samuel, an Ephraimite or Was He a Levite as Indicated in 1 Chronicles 6:16–30?* 2014. http://defendinginerrancy.com/bible-solutions/1_Samuel_1.1.php.

———. *Judges 18:30—How Could This Book Have Been Written in the Time or Shortly After the Time of the Judges?* 2014. http://defendinginerrancy.com/bible-solutions/Judges_18.30.php.

———. *Matthew 1:17—How Many Generations Were Listed Between the Captivity and Christ, 14 or 13?* 2014. http://defendinginerrancy.com/bible-solutions/Matthew_1.17.php.

———. *Matthew 1:8—Is Joram the Father of Uzziah or of Ahaziah?* 2014. http://defendinginerrancy.com/bible-solutions/Matthew_1.8.php.

Giles, Kevin. *Justifying Injustice with the Bible: Apartheid*. 2016. https://www.cbeinternational.org/blogs/justifying-injustice-bible-apartheid.

Gonzalez, Justo L. *The Story of Christianity, Volume 1*. Peabody, MS: Prince, 1984.

Grudem, Wayne. *Why Voting for Donald Trump is a Morally Good Choice*. 2016. https://townhall.com/columnists/waynegrudem/2016/07/28/why-voting-for-donald-trump-is-a-morally-good-choice-n2199564.

Gundry, Robert H. *Matthew: A Commentary on His Literary and Theological Art*. Grand Rapids, MI: Eerdmans, 1982.

———. *Smithereens! Bible-reading and "Pervasive Interpretive Pluralism."* 2011. https://www.booksandculture.com/articles/2011/sepoct/smithreens.html.

Haddon, Mark. *The Curious Incident of the Dog in the Night-time*. New York: Vintage, 2003.

Holding, James P. *Sargon vs Moses*. 2013. http://www.tektonics.org/copycat/sargon.php.

Hübner, Jamin A. *Adventures in Sexist Hermeneutics*. 2017. https://www.youtube.com/watch?v=8EDMoDAF3BI.

Jewish Women's Archive. *Telling Stories, Discovering Midrash, and Learning about Lilith—Lesson Plan for Families*. https://jwa.org/teach/golearn/sep07/family (accessed September 21, 2018).

Johnson, D. H. "Life." In *New Dictionary of Biblical Theology*, edited by T. Desmond Alexander and Brian S. Rosner. Downers Grove, IL: IVP, 2000.

Jones, Robert P., and Daniel Cox. *Backing Trump, White Evangelicals Flip Flop on Importance of Candidate Character | PRRI/Brookings Survey*. 2016. http://www.prri.org/research/prri-brookings-oct-19-poll-politics-election-clinton-double-digit-lead-trump/.

Khazan, Olga. *Inside the Mind of a Hypocrite: Why Hypocrisy Bothers us So Much, and How Politicians Can Rationalize it Anyway*. 2017. https://www.theatlantic.com/science/archive/2017/06/mind-of-a-hypocrite/530958/.

King, Martin Luther. *Letter from Birmingham Jail*. 1963. https://web.cn.edu/kwheeler/documents/Letter_Birmingham_Jail.pdf.

Kolbert, Elizabeth. *Why Facts don't Change Our Minds: New Discoveries about the Human Mind Show the Limitations of Reason*. 2017. https://www.newyorker.com/magazine/2017/02/27/why-facts-dont-change-our-minds.

Kovacs, Maureen G. *The Epic of Gilgamesh: Tablet XI: The Story of the Flood.* 1998. http://www.ancienttexts.org/library/mesopotamian/gilgamesh/tab11.htm.

Kruglanski, Arie W., and Edward Orehek. *The Need for Certainty as a Psychological Nexus for Individuals and Society.* 2011. https://www.researchgate.net/publication/230395124_The_Need_for_Certainty_as_a_Psychological_Nexus_for_Individuals_and_Society.

Kurtzleben, Danielle. *White Evangelicals have Warmed to Politicians who Commit 'Immoral' Acts.* 2016. https://www.npr.org/2016/10/23/498890836/poll-white-evangelicals-have-warmed-to-politicians-who-commit-immoral-acts.

Lewis, C. S. *Mere Christianity.* San Francisco, CA: HarperCollins, 2001.

Long, V. Philips. *The Art of Biblical History.* Leicester: Apollos, 1994.

Mantzavinos, C. *Hermeneutics.* 2016. https://plato.stanford.edu/entries/hermeneutics/.

McArthur, John. *The Statement on Social Justice and the Gospel.* 2018. https://statementonsocialjustice.com/.

McCulloch, Sarah. *List of Hebrew Bible Books by Length.* 2012. http://www.sarahmcculloch.com/religion/2012/list-hebrew-bible-books-length/.

McIntire, C. T. "Fundamentalism." In *Evangelical Dictionary of Theology*, edited by Walter A. Elwell, 472–5. Grand Rapids, MI: Baker Academic, 2001.

Merrick, J., and Stephen M. Garrett. "Introduction: On Debating Inerrancy." In *Five Views on Biblical Inerrancy*, edited by J. Merrick and Stephen M. Garrett, 9–28. Grand Rapids, MI: Zondervan, 2013.

More in Common. *The Hidden Tribes of America.* 2018. https://hiddentribes.us/.

Olson, Roger. *What is "Fundamentalism"?* 2017. https://www.patheos.com/blogs/rogereolson/2017/08/what-is-fundamentalism/.

Packer, J. I. *"Fundamentalism" and the Word of God.* Leicester: IVP, 1958.

———. "Liberalism and Conservativism in Theology." In *New Dictionary of Theology*, edited by Sinclair B Ferguson and J I Packer, 384–5. Downers Grove, IL: IVP, 2000.

Philips, Emo. *The Best God Joke Ever – and it's Mine!* 2005. https://www.theguardian.com/stage/2005/sep/29/comedy.religion.

Pickering, Jordan. *Friendly Racism.* 2017. https://longwind.wordpress.com/2017/11/16/friendly-racism/.

———. *Pee Pastor an Example to the Rest of Us.* 2010. https://longwind.wordpress.com/2010/01/27/pee_pastor/.

Pierard, Richard V., and Walter A. Elwell. "Evangelicalism." In *Evangelical Dictionary of Theology*, edited by Walter A. Elwell, 405–410. Grand Rapids, MI: Baker Academic, 2001.

Rock, David. *A Hunger for Certainty.* 2009. https://www.psychologytoday.com/us/blog/your-brain-work/200910/hunger-certainty.

Sanders, E. P. *Jesus and Judaism.* Minneapolis, MN: Fortress, 1985.

Seely, Paul H. "The Firmament and the Water Above, Part I." 2009. *Westminster Theological Journal* 53 (1991) 227–40. https://faculty.gordon.edu/hu/bi/ted_hildebrandt/otesources/01-genesis/text/articles-books/seely-firmament-wtj.pdf.

Smith, Christian. *The Bible Made Impossible: Why Biblicism is not a Truly Evangelical Reading of Scripture.* Grand Rapids, MI: Brazos, 2011.

Sproul, R. C. *Do we Believe the Whole Gospel?* 2010. https://www.ligonier.org/learn/articles/do-we-believe-whole-gospel/.

Swedenborg, Emmanuel. *Arcana Coelestia, Volume 1.* 1749. https://books.google.co.za/books?id=TcMCAgAAQBAJ.

Thiselton, Anthony. *Hermeneutics: An Introduction.* Grand Rapids, MI: Eerdmans, 2009.

# Bibliography

Thomas, Emily. *Does the Size of the Universe Prove God Doesn't Exist?* 2017. http://theconversation.com/does-the-size-of-the-universe-prove-god-doesnt-exist-86645.

Van Seters, John. *Prologue to History: The Yahwist as Historian in Genesis.* Louisville, KY: Westminster / John Knox, 1992.

Von Rad, Gerhard. *Genesis: A Commentary.* Revised. Translated by John H. Marks and John Bowden. London: SCM Press, 1972.

Waldman, Paul. *Republicans Reach Staggering New Heights of Hypocrisy.* 2017. https://www.washingtonpost.com/blogs/plum-line/wp/2017/01/06/republicans-reach-staggering-new-heights-of-hypocrisy.

Walton, John H. "A Historical Adam: Archetypal Creation View." In *Four Views on the Historical Adam*, edited by Matthew M. Barrett and Ardel B. Caneday, 89–118. Grand Rapids, MI: Zondervan, 2013.

Weekly Standard. *Great Moments in Liberal Hypocrisy.* 2016. https://www.weeklystandard.com/the-scrapbook/great-moments-in-liberal-hypocrisy.

Witherington, Ben. *Martin vs. Barton on Historical Criticism and the Issue of Meaning.* 2009. http://benwitherington.blogspot.com/2009/01/martin-vs-barton-on-historical.html.

Woodbridge, John D. *Biblical Authority: A Critique of the Rogers/McKim Proposal.* Grand Rapids, MI: Zondervan, 1982.

Wootson, Cleve R. *Fox News's Laura Ingraham says Immigrant Child Detention Centers are 'Essentially Summer Camps'.* 2018. https://www.washingtonpost.com/news/arts-and-entertainment/wp/2018/06/19/fox-news-laura-ingraham-says-immigrant-child-detention-centers-are-essentially-summer-camps/.

Zylstra, Sarah E. *Dobson Explains why he Called Trump a 'Baby Christian.'* 2016. https://www.christianitytoday.com/news/2016/august/james-dobson-explains-why-donald-trump-baby-christian.html.

www.ingramcontent.com/pod-product-compliance
Lightning Source LLC
Chambersburg PA
CBHW071451150426
43191CB00008B/1305